The M the Na

The astonishing illustrated story of how a mind was dismantled and repaired

John Smale

Based on true events

AN IMPORTANT NOTE FOR THE READER

There are pictures to illustrate some of the scenarios that Adam Rice found himself in for the benefit of the reader. Some of these are nude pictures. They are not for titillation but represent the images in the imagination and fantasy of a troubled man obsessed with domination and control of others.

There are also descriptions of abuse and violence and so may not be suitable for the sensitive.

Published in January 2015 by emp3books Ltd
Norwood House, Elvetham Road, Fleet, GU51 4HL

©John Smale 2015

ISBN-13: 978-1-907140-97-6

Contents

Forward

Many readers will not believe that the following really happened. I did not at first. However it is based on the authentic experiences of a genuinely discontented man.

The following narrative tells of a primal form of healing where spirits represent the causes of mental problems and the inability to cope with what life throws at us.

As a therapist of many years experience I realised that it is necessary to go back to the dark rooms of the past and to open the black cupboards that contain the crap that has changed a person for the worse.

This account comes from a man who told me his story in order to help others rather than seek help from me. I have transcribed it as best as possible from the notes I made with inputs from Adam Rice (not his real name to preserve privacy) who undertook the journey.

The pictures were chosen by him as being the closest approximation of what he remembers seeing.

Sometimes, some forms of therapy are spontaneous, unexpected and less formal than psychotherapy as it is known in our present times.

There is an old therapy that uses metaphors to enable us to deal with the mental demons that live inside our heads. The cave dwelling shamans of old were the first to use this form of psychotherapy to find a release from the malevolence that wrecks lives.

Adam Rice is a man whose life was totally destroyed by his desire for money, women and power. This resulted in major unhappiness at not always getting what he wanted.

Almost as a joke he thought he would take part in an old style of ritual that would give him knowledge of the paranormal that would empower him to get what he considered necessary for his complete happiness.

How wrong that thought was in intention but not in its result. It involved a journey through the dark places in his mind that terrified him but which brought about a change that affected everything in his life.

These changes are summarised in a separate section in the second half of the book written by Adam for the benefit of others.

Dark

Dark

Not the dark of darkness

The dark of death

Nothingness

Adam was unaware of where he was as he tumbled down a long tunnel into darkness.

His body seemed to bounce off the walls but he felt no pain. He looked for clues as to where he was. There had been no slopes or holes before.

With our eyes closed we can see nothing. Perhaps there is an awareness of the light outside but there are no images.

When we dream the view is clear. We are able to perceive everything in colour and in all dimensions.

Adam was in total darkness so this was no dream, just a blindness that was impenetrable.

"I must be dead." He thought.

"I cannot smell, feel or hear anything.

"My brain has closed down.

"But there again, I can think these thoughts.

"I can question my state of nothingness.

"But I can't figure out why this depth of feeling of total emptiness has a setting in my conscious mind.

"Reason tells me to feel around to make contact with a solid base, side or top.

"Nevertheless there is nothing.

"I try to hear something, even the pulsing of my blood in my ears.

"Still nothing."

He tested his five senses; sight, hearing, touch, taste and smell.

"Yet, still bloody nothing.

"It is as if I am a thinking brain devoid of a connection to a mechanical means of transportation.

"But I feel fear. Is that physical sense?

"No. It is from my emotions. They are feelings created in the mind and they prompt the body into action.

"Or does it work the other way?

"Does the body provoke emotions that instruct the mind to make the body run?

"Maybe, but anyway I have no body that I am aware of."

His unforeseen arrival in this place came from a choice he had made to visit a new age style event that involved taking part in a sweat lodge.

Like a reality show on the television he knew that he would have to suffer in order to gain. And his prize was unthinkable at this stage.

The Dawn of Darkness

On that Saturday evening, as naked as the day on which he was born, Adam stood in the middle of a field with eight other people making a circle around the crackling fire. Some were dancing around and chanting as if to bring the primeval world into that place.

He had undressed with reserve earlier as had the other participants.

Looking around in the dim light he established that men and women made equal numbers. They shared a range of ages.

Adam's journey had begun with a visit to a shamanic sweat lodge and there, unwittingly, his soul seemed to have become stuck in a place where his nightmares came to him for solutions.

Adam had reviewed the women for any that might be of interest to his libido. One in particular caught his eye but she seemed detached and he had no apparent appeal to her.

He was proud of his thirty two year old body. He ran three or four times every week, partly for fitness but mainly to use his body and looks as a mobile sandwich board to be seen by admiring spectators. He was not over tall but his padded trainers added a little height as he jogged along.

He would smile at women as he ran past and hoped they would respond. Some did but mostly they were caught up in their own races with life. Getting to work, scurrying to collect schoolchildren or rushing to the shops

Now around this bright fire he scanned the naked female bodies. Adam felt happy that he had chosen a good place to be. In the ambiguous light offered by the fire at sunset some of them were pleasant to look at, others not, but this was never meant to be a fashion event. This was not a catalogue from which to choose a lover.

With his heart beating in time to the drum, he was embarrassed and cynical but like a person strapped into a roller coaster ride, he had no choice but to continue.

Crawling slowly, one by one, they all went through the small entrance of the branch and mud construction. Moving around the circular earth bank that doubled as a bench he sat where he was instructed by the shaman. He closed his eyes and felt his body rebelling at the anticipation of the experience.

When they were all settled, the canvas flap that acted as the door was closed. The leader of this venture said some prayers which meant little to Adam and called for the lava stones that had been heating over the fire.

In the dark their red glow made them alarming rather than comforting as a warm fire glowing in a hearth would have been at home. They had been told that these stones were used because they would not crack and spit hot splinters when water was poured over them.

After being brought, the rocks were placed in a small pit in the middle of this gloomy space. Water was slowly dribbled onto them. It hissed briefly at the pain. The heat and steam soured upwards and outwards so that Adam had to catch his breath.

The heat was intense. Adam's whole nature was resisting the extreme stress that it was encountering. His body produced copious amounts of sweat in an attempt to cope. It flowed out of his skin as a warm flood.

The high temperatures and humidity made a Swedish sauna seem like a comfortable place to be.

The heat and the smell of the hot wooden frame plus the aroma of the sage that had been used to sanitise the lodge combined with the intense odour of perspiration and started to make his mind feel fuzzy.

As instructed, as a novice, he prayed to the East, the South, the West and the North.

And then to the elements of Earth, Fire, Air and Water.

Then to his ancestors.

11

Feeling foolish and totally out of his depth Adam followed the shaman's instructions to make his personal entreaty to the universe.

He pondered hard, and partly from desperation, he asked for the resolution of all of his problems, hoping that this was general enough to give strength and power to his selfish need for pleasure and then he sat for a while, flicking sweat from his chest with his hand, to let this request sink in.

He rested in that place but then he found himself disappearing into a dizzy and blank haze.

Giddiness...

Wooziness...

Faintness...

Panicking, he worried that this was the onset on his death.

He had no control of his fate. It was as if he was being taken over and taken away. He decided to make his exit from this cramped and scorching space.

Leaving that hot enclosed place on his hands and knees Adam gulped in the cooler air, stood up slowly and attempted to retrieve his discarded clothes from the pile he had left them in.

As he reached out, he staggered around before he passed out. He fell face first to the earth and plummeted, deeper and deeper, into a new and very, very dark world with his fingers stretched out as if reaching for rescue. They clutched desperately in so much panic that the tendons locked tightly making his hands look like the talons of a bird of prey about to capture its victim.

He was dead, he was sure.

The Brink of Sanity

After he had stopped rolling and bouncing, Adam's vision grabbed a glimmer of light and a new apparition opened in front of his eyes.

He could see the entrance to a small and narrow cave in front of him.

It was either real or something that he saw with his imagination, but every picture we see with our eyes is constructed by our brains anyway, he knew.

There were rocks of every colour funnelling into darkness.

Yet, to Adam this seemed as if he was looking at a part of his brain rather than a grotto. It was familiar to him for some reason.

He was surprised as he was able to enter the cave even though it seemed tiny. "Yet if I have no body, then I can go anywhere I want. I can fit into the smallest nook and cranny." He thought.

He squeezed through the entrance and entered a long passage with a feeling of claustrophobia as the walls pressed in on him.

As a stark contrast, once he passed through the dark channel the interior had a bright ruddy hue but at that moment he could not focus on anything. As he entered the space the entrance appeared to close behind him.

A regular thud was beating in his ears. The sound was making him more anxious about where he was and what he would be subjected to. "Well, at least, I can hear as well as see." He muttered to himself quietly.

His hands were chilly although sweaty and his heart seemed to be pounding in time to the beat.

"So I do have a heart."

Bump, bump, bump, bump, bump, bump, bump, bump, bump, bump...It thumped in time to the noise.

Confused by the repetitive sound, Adam closed his eyes to allow his mind to comprehend the meaning of that sinister feeling he was experiencing.

He sensed an unease about what had brought him here but his mind was blank and seemed only receptive to what was in front of him.

The sweet flower like smell was fighting with rank stenches. His mouth was full of mucus and he found it difficult to swallow. He wanted to stop but something, his instinct for survival, was telling him it was necessary to continue to the end because he was stuck wherever he was, or thought he was.

All he could see was a red dome surrounding him, trapping him in an enclosed space.

Then there was just silence, there was no noise.

The blurred scene started to clear.

"But if this noise, smell and sight are in my imagination then perhaps I can change them to what I need them to be.

"Yet I could be locked into a chain of events as I have been in dreams where my sleeping mind puts me into situations that I have no control of, but which worry me when I wake."

He was lost and confused. Yet, after all, he made the decision to go into the sweat lodge in an attempt to see behind that murky barrier in his life to find what had been hidden for so long, the resolve of his anxious state in life. He seemed to have no choice but to continue to discover how this story would unfold.

There was silence again. Imagine total silence. Difficult.

Then his new world dissolved into nothingness.

Bare Facts

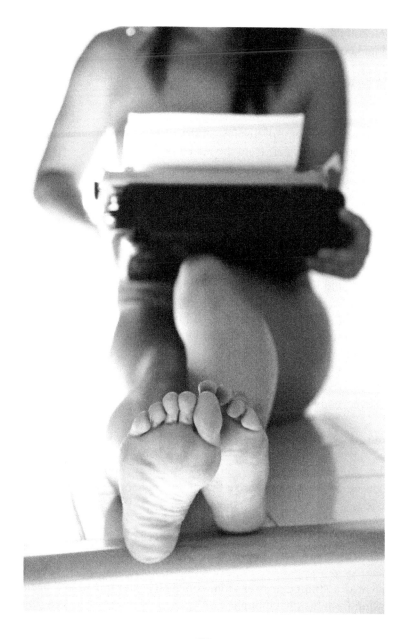

Tap, tap, tap on a typewriter.

The sharp noises rang out.

Somebody seemed to be writing the story of Adam's life so far. How did he know that?

Words were pouring out from the keys as if he was making a confession from the soul that resided inside him.

His secrets were on full display on the screen for all to read but there was nobody there apart from the naked typist.

Strange. Where did she come from? And why?

"Dictate the story of your life." She demanded with a voice like a Gestapo officer mixed with the beautiful buxom blond she appeared to be.

"Why should I?" Adam replied, feeling grilled by this stranger.

She continued typing. "Alright. I will type it as it is anyway. It might be different to what you remember but it will tell it as it is."

"To whom?"

"To everybody who wants to know."

"And who might they be?"

"The people who have formed an opinion of you in the past who might be persuaded to change their minds when they hear your point of view.

"And, to be fair you might change your ideas about them when you become aware of what they think."

That was a strange answer from somebody who must have been an illusion from his own thoughts.

Adam scrutinized her body. Pale, smooth skin and pert breasts. Yet she had a look that scared him to the core.

Even so, he assessed her suitability for sex as if he were an opportunist boss trying to have an affair with his personal assistant.

"This is a strange fantasy." He thought.

He looked away, confused and a little shocked.

"Where am I and who are you?" He asked with a tone of fear in his voice. His hands shivered as he felt more lost in this nightmare land that he had become involved in as he sought the reality of his situation in his confused mind.

As if she was a high court judge, she delivered her verdict.

"You will now read and experience the events, thoughts and actions in your life episode by episode as the truth transforms into solid words from your memories. They need to be amended in order for you to achieve what you asked for, happiness."

As an additional rebuke, she continued. "The joys of life that you had experienced before you came here were as illusionary as the place in your mind that you are in now."

She stared at Adam with a look on her face that resembled the look a doctor has when he gives patients the news that they have a terminal disease

Adam remained confused but the truth would begin to dawn on him soon.

The Naked Truth

Adam was still nude and floating in the cave. He was not concerned because there was nobody there now to see him in the darkness apart from the clerk who was as naked as he was.

Missing his Armani suits, he felt as exposed as the emperor in his invisible clothes being gawped at and ridiculed by the crowd.

"So what have you written so far?" He asked.

"Well," she replied, "your first evaluation of me was in looking at my exposed body. Rather than trying to find out who I am. You wanted to see if I was of sexual interest, an object of desire, and that depended upon which portion of me you looked at. That was the most important aspect of me for you on our first meeting. Here you are in a strange place, not knowing anything about your situation but you still want to decide whether I would be good to touch and to have sex with. That is one of the many ways in which you have upset people in your life."

As if by magic, suddenly the clerk is fully clothed and sitting up straight.

"Does that help you to think more clearly?"

"Not really. I can still imagine your undressed body when I look at you."

He was deliberately being rude to this person who had some sort of power because she was in a position of dominance over his life that he had no control of.

"How about now?" The clerk was naked again but with the body of a very, very old wrinkly person with no gender clues.

"So are you now a man or a woman or something moulded by a Thai surgeon to be a ladyboy?" He asked sarcastically to her unisex old body.

She stared at Adam with judgement in her questioning eyes.

He wanted to emphasize his sexual orientation to this enigma. "I am a single gendered person. I am a man."

"But your mother is female and your father male. That makes you a fusion of both." A stern tone was in the voice. "I am a mixture of man and woman as you are. You see me as you wish to see me."

"What is your point?" He asked, almost demanded.

"Throughout your life you wanted people for your sexual pleasure and relief. You made love very rarely but fucked often. Did you ever think about how much pain your self-centred pleasure cost?

"You enticed women into your life as if you were setting mouse traps. Your charm and your promises were the cheese that lured. Once caught they were hurt or injured by your lack of regard for their feelings. You wanted beautiful bodies as a butterfly collector wants those glorious insects. They catch them, kill them and then pin them to boards for their own gratification. The dead give happiness to the hoarders of exquisiteness that cannot share life with others because their lives have been broken. If they could speak they would have nothing but contempt for the thieves of their magnificence and the despoilers of their emotions."

She paused for a while and resumed.

"You used your sexual partners rather than attempting to share a loving relationship. You took without giving anything back. You left them feeling used, abused and dirty while you only had a sense of pride and satisfaction in your seduction."

Shocked by her language and tone, Adam felt as if he was being stretched on a rack of guilt.

Suddenly, the cave's light changed and he was aware of the apparition of other people. It was as if a whole cast of shadowy extras had marched onto the stage.

There were lots of exhausted and hurt bodies forming around him. A fusion of his victims and a jury. They were pointing fingers at him and sneering. He was ignorant of the beauty that he had once craved through the distortion of disdain and loathing.

Lost for something to do or say he just managed to utter "I am sorry." His voice was weak and feeble.

Sometimes apologies are insincere and they attempt to cover the cracks but those few words were heartfelt.
He was able to see people beyond the flush of personal joy after he was relieved of his sexual need. No afterglow, only remorse.

Their tears stopped and his started until he was wet all over as he had been in the sweat lodge from his perspiration.

They, rather than being happy at the joy of retribution, withdrew with the look of disappointment in the person, Adam, who had used them.

They only felt contempt for him. That hurt him.

Like a choir of angry people the voices of those women came together to terminate the meeting.

"Love making is a mutual pleasure because the sharing of bodies is satisfaction for both parties. Sex, however can be one sided. If one partner demands sex for their own relief then the other person is left feeling used. That emotion of being exploited will return to the user in different ways.

"If love making cannot be a shared joy then it is necessary to find out why one person is eating the whole pizza and drinking the whole bottle of wine."

As they disappeared into a mist the voice of the clerk returned.

"And on a similar subject, you screwed people financially as well. Your gain, their loss. You used their skills to make money for you without any reward for them. You never worried that the time they spent working was subtracted from the time they should have spent with their families and in leisure. They were nothing but slaves and if they ever complained then you fired them. Perhaps I will call them to reveal their hurt later."

Adam's apprehension increased. This had not turned out to be a pleasurable experience.

"By the way, did you not realise that the cave entrance you entered resembles the entrance to a vagina? You have spent so much of your life trying to get into them and now that your whole body has returned to the place where you were conceived and born from, you seem uncomfortable." Her mocking smile burnt into him like a red hot poker.

The cave had changed. Not in the way of a film with expensive special effects but more like an amateur dramatic play in a village hall with badly made scenery.

Red and bloody, this huge palpating womb now contained the torture that he had given to other people being returned to him in a grotesque way.

Then, neither attractive nor repulsive, the body started to become transparent and the shape melted into the incomprehensible and the totally surreal place Adam was lost in.

Light was now flooding in as a landscape came into being like an old photographic plate developing.

Lost in the Wild

Adam was now in a wilderness as if he had been returned to the days of his cave dwelling ancestors. It was as if his embryonic self was going back in time rather than growing to maturity.

The departure from the dark chasm had taken him into barren wasteland.

Bare brown and dusty scrubland. The ground was a mass of low mounds that progressed outwards from the cave in the cliff which he must have exited.

Brushing off pieces of spider web stuck to the slime on his body, he lurched into this new landscape.

He was in a wide space which was as big as his mind could make, but his imagination had no limits. The sky was blue and the sun was beating down with the intensity of a spotlight. It felt like a wonderful change to the scene he had left, but only for the moment.

Thirsty, Adam stumbled to a pool of water. He drank from a cup that was laying there. Once he had sated his dryness he threw the cup away and started to explore this new place.

To his total horror, this hot and inhospitable place he was in was full of snakes, spiders and scorpions.

Some people love snakes. Adam felt comfortable with small constrictors but he was scared of the venomous ones. They can be quick, strike if upset and will kill with their poison given half a chance.

He was tight with fear; his heart beating so fast that it hurt. He wanted to run but there was nowhere safe to go.

Then the black scorpions, rat sized, appeared closer to him. Clicking their claws, they were looking at Adam with their array of eyes as if he was their greatest enemy. Staring and inching forward they had so much menace that he wanted to shout out with fear even though there was nobody there to hear him.

He was terrified. He had fought with big men in a boxing ring. He knew what to do, knew how to punch, head-butt, kick and hurt. But scorpions and snakes were alien to his protective instincts. They represented pure danger.

A black lobster shaped monster scurried towards his bare feet. He could not run or move without stepping on more of them or getting close to the strike of a rattler.

Pain. Agonising red hot pain rushed into his foot, calf, thigh and body.

Adam collapsed. This was not the departure from the mayhem that he wanted.

The scorpion's barb withdrew and dribbles of its venom were flowing, gushing, out of the wound and its curved stinger.

He opened his eyes. It burned; it tingled within his swelling flesh. Panicking at the thought of his impending death, he looked around as if searching for an antidote that surely did not exist there.

Then, tall and elegant in her fur clothes, a primordial woman was standing next to him. With dark, curly hair, almost medusa like at first glance, she stood holding a wooden staff in her hand. Strangely, he hardly noticed that she was scantily dressed in furs. Although he abhorred fur clothing he, without thinking, accepted that this had come with her way of primeval life.

He was aware of her beauty but this was a chance for rescue rather than an opportunity for desire.

"Fear." He heard a soft voice say, "That is what lots of people felt when you were around them. Fear from you controlling their lives financially, emotionally and physically. These creatures represent the dread that people felt in your presence. The cup you threw away earlier was the way you treated your female conquests and your employees. Once used and then discarded."

"Shit." Adam bellowed. "Another evaluator." He wanted to be

rescued rather than condemned.

She ignored his comment.

"After you had satisfied your thirst you had no need of the vessel you used and disposed of it. You knew you would find another when you needed to drink.

"The scorpion stabbed you or you thought it did. You have no body; you have left no footprints in the sand.

"Now you are a free soul that can float through the world and evaluate what has happened in your life. Its poison is not a magical potion but something that will hold your body still while your spirit travels further onwards."

"And who are you?" Adam's voice was pleading rather than questioning to this new person in his frenzied state of mind.

"I am a guardian and a reviewer who will guide you through the continuation of the journey you will undertake. You can think of me as your guide through the areas of your thoughts you might wish to ride over."

"Like a fairy godmother." There was no humour meant but Adam was disturbed and confused.

Exhausted from this barrage of truth and potential judgement, he felt no sense of malice from her but he still wanted to escape from this forbidding fairytale.

Biting Your Tongue

Adam was nothing now. No limbs, no body but he floated around, invisible to the real world and he had to go where he was directed.

It was like having a dream where we take part in things, witness events and interact with others while our bodies are laying in our beds.

The difference was that he was being guided to where he had to go and like in a nightmare; he had no control and no sense of choice, only an intense dread of the next event.

These were moments that mixed terror with exploration.

The adventurers in the world must have felt the same when they were sailing oceans in search of new lands and then perhaps meeting hostile natives who wanted to eliminate the invaders of their territories. The same would apply to mountain climbers, deep sea divers and astronauts facing unidentified threats. The unknown is daunting as well as intriguing.

Back in the ether of uncertainty he realised that the demons he must face were created in his own life by himself.

As well as having awareness of the people he had mistreated Adam remembered the wicked people he had met in his own existence.

The guide told him that it was necessary to bring them into that special place and to prepare to deal with them.

The thought appealed to him. The tables were turning away from the constant criticism he had received so far.

Those scary creations that are in fairy tales were based on real people like the ones he had known.

He hovered above a sickening school teacher who had taken no interest in him as a pupil. That man implied that Adam had no intelligence and that he was wasting his time.

"You nasty bastard." He shouted, "You didn't like a pupil who asked

questions that you thought threatened your sense of superiority."
There is no reaction. Adam's voice was not heard, his presence not
felt nor seen.

"What is the point of this?" He asked his guide.

"Reliving those events with extra knowledge you did not possess
before will allow you to gain a different point of view and it should
explain some of your inbuilt resentment of authority figures."

He and the guide floated to the teacher's house. Adam witnessed that
he had a bad home life. His wife was lazy but had a sizzling love life
outside the marriage and a frigid one within it.

The teacher's frustration, hurt and annoyance were reassigned to
people over whom he thought he had control and who were unable to
fight back. His lack of influence at home had to be replaced by
dominance over his charges in the classroom. Nobody could condone
that but with new insight his behaviour could be understood.

It became clear to Adam that he enjoyed controlling others because
he lacked control of certain things in his own life.

The scene was changing. Perhaps he had sought revenge on the few
partners who used him while they were taking his love and money.
Those people were real and he had to take the malevolence that they
spawned.

Yet, it seemed to him that they might have been seeking retribution
for the way Adam had treated them. Floating above women who
were familiar to him, he could see the hurt he had given for his use of
their bodies rather than the beauty of the love that they had wanted to
share rather than give. There were not that many, he never was a
Casanova but he had taken his small pieces of what he thought was
pleasure at the time.

Following them after his departures from intimacy, he could see the
tears they shed having been used for sex rather than making love.
The grinding and grunting he did was an insult. It could have been
any woman laying there giving her body to pleasure just him. After

all, they had seemed the same in bed with his eyes closed. Blinded by his requirements he never tried to discover their needs and desires.

They were nothing but soft, sweet smelling bodies of flesh that were there for his enjoyment. The gap between physical and emotional satisfaction had been far too wide for him to comprehend at those times.

The difference between rape and what he did to some women is hard to define. At least at the beginning they had been willing and agreeable but afterwards they would have felt violated by his lack of concern and lack of interest in them.

This journey was becoming one huge expedition that was examining his self-interests, bigoted views and inability to recognise his failings as a human.

He was plunging deeper into his dark thoughts of mistreatment.

And then the guide said "Enter the confessional, Adam."

A Loss from Profit

As well as his sexual partners there was still the mistreatment of the people he had worked with to be taken into consideration.

When Adam considered his transgressions in his business life he was reminded of the lives he had hurt and destroyed.

He became aware of the aftermath of unemployed people who had done their best, but never to the level of profit making that he wanted for himself. So he fired them.

Now he had to watch as those people went home to tell their husbands, wives or partners that they had lost their jobs.

Adam had not considered that being blinkered in his sight he had been unable to see how losing a piece from a jigsaw made the whole puzzle worthless, not only for his businesses but for the individual lives involved.

Like a Roman emperor just one thumbs-down meant a proverbial loss of living for a man or woman.

Adam objected this outsider's view of his professional life.

The guide jumped in. "What is happening to you at this moment is instruction on how to stop making mistakes and learning how to live your live benevolently. Had you taken the time and effort needed to teach skills and techniques to those poor workers you used and fired, then you might have gained far more from a grateful and motivated member of staff, even apart from the cost of recruiting and training their replacements.

"Cutting off noses to spite faces has happened through history. It can only be assumed that you did badly at becoming skilled at the management and support of your staff.

"You made mistakes in you early career, Adam. Yet you were lucky enough to have bosses who could see potential through the haze of the errors you made.

Then he was conscious of other bosses who promoted their own interests rather than the people who could achieve results. He was in the boardrooms where the men and women argued about profitability and waste while they calculated what a better bottom line would do to their bonuses.

They treated the employees as resources, an ironic word, Adam thought. Resources are things that are used for profit and which are used up and replaced for the benefit of the user. Slaves would be a better word.

Adam spoke aloud. "Human Resources is a term that should be dumped for its implication of servitude and subjugation. By following those bosses into their private lives it once again showed patterns that were reflected at work.

"I can see that their insecurity, their mortgage payments, their unhappy relationships and more drove them to adopt the personas of strength and dominance that would catalyse their moral beliefs into those of a despot. They were always in a larger spotlight than those they employed and had to act like generals fighting far from the front line, using cannon fodder to save their own skins.

"If they had better lives in private they might have been better bosses.

"Very logical, but to my mind, still unforgivable.

"And besides, some of them were just nasty pieces of work."

The guide let out a sigh of relief.

Adam knew that he had been one of them without too much sense of right and wrong, just self interest.

That applied to many areas of his life he now knew.

False Beliefs

As if appearing from a magician's puff of smoke, Adam became aware of a man, robed as a holy person standing in front of him. He looked as intimidating as a horror film character.

But we are not into a book about fictional children's' stories complete with spooky witches and wizards. We are in Adam's own head, in his personal space that was bursting at the seams with frightening memories.

There he was, in a dark abyss that seemed as sinister as his guilty conscience. He had no idea to whom, and what he was supposed to be confessing.

Belief befuddles the mind. It dictates the way in which we live. It delegates the power we should have over our lives to others who want to claim it. Religious fervour muddles and confuses us.

And that control comes from fear.

Ironically fear comes from the power that is used to make people do what they do not want to do in order to avoid those things that they do not want happening to them.

When we believe in magic we ignore the trickery that is involved. Likewise miracles are holy powers that can lead people to believe in an extraordinary influence that can change the unchangeable and will be used against us if we do not behave ourselves.

Just because people go to church on Sundays it does not mean that they are good folk.

Perhaps some are trying to flush away their own self doubts and guilt. Others want to be in command with their holy power being the weapon.

Anyway, Adam was in the church that he went to as a child. The smell of incense filled the air along with a dusty, very old and damp odour.

Alarm rather than salvation is what he felt. An indefinable sense of foreboding saturated the air.

There was the man, Father Hugh, dressed in his apparel. He was the priest who liked to touch young boys. He told them that it was to save their souls and that God would forgive their sins if they did certain things to him and allowed him to do things to those young boys.

He told them that they must keep it a secret or they would be punished by the Devil and they would go to a fiery Hell where they would burn for eternity. To demonstrate his point he burnt their arms in places that would not show up to their parents with candles so these youngsters could feel what Hell was like.

He worked on the principle that if a boy had enough faith to go to church then he would also believe in the representative of the Deity, him.

Adam's choice apparently, at that point was to do something that he did not want to do, go to Hell or tell his mother. He wished that Father Hugh would go away and leave the kids in peace.

He would adopt an authoritarian pose, pace around the lads and beat a stick against his hand. Everything was done to create a figure of supremacy and secret supernatural knowledge.

One day, fortunately, Adam's mother arrived at the point when he was to be made to make a choice between being abused or to burn in Hades. His brother had tripped and broken his leg. He had to go home. Apologies were made to the priest and his mum took him away.

A few days later it was announced that Father Hugh had died from a heart attack.

Although relieved and feeling guilty for such, he asked his mother why God had allowed a priest to die.

"Ah. He has gone to Heaven to be at rest. He was a good man who committed no sins and was loved by everybody, son."

41

From his new vantage point in this strange dream he could see that he had been a dirty old man, a paedophile who knew that what he was doing was a sin and that, according to him, would definitely prohibit him from going anywhere but to a bad place where he would be an eternal human candle for the Devil with his penis as the wick.

He obviously had no belief in anything apart from the power of his status to enable him to do what he wanted by using fear to coerce his victims into giving him his joy.

"Rest in flames, Father Hugh." Adam shouted loudly.

The shamanic guide had a look on her face to say that although she could not influence outcomes in the real world, maybe she operated as a Guardian Angel in his very early years to save him from the evil priest's clutches, even if it meant breaking his brother's leg!

Adam remembered that there was still a lot of work to be done to rid the world of men, and women, who have the same perverted streak of selfish malevolence in them.

"Can you do the same to all the other wicked bastards, please?" His pleading question was answered in a cryptic way.

"Remember that they will be brought to account when the time is right."

Adam was sure he heard a scathing laugh after this hint of an afterlife that is judgemental.

"If only Hell existed." He screamed into the void.

"It does." Was the guide's reply, softly spoken.

Silence followed for a while until something even more shocking happened.

Hell

Flames shot up and around. There was heat but Adam had no body to burn, nevertheless the nightmare existed in front of his eyes.

"Adam. You will see visions of Hell, not as in the threat of the priest but as it exists on Earth. You are innocent of what you will see but only to the extent that your hurt has not gone as far as what you will witness. The thing to remember is that whether a pain is small or large, they will hurt just the same at that moment. A small ice pick through the brain does as much harm as a huge axe.

We will open the pages one by one."

Adam knew this would not be a cheerful event like finding chocolate in an advent calendar but it would be like an array of evil people being released from a top-security psychiatric prison.

He was frozen in fear, nervousness and trepidation even as the flames licked around him. If he had bowels they would have emptied in a flash.

A Pound of Flesh

Adam saw the revolting sexual abuse of women and children that he was unable to describe without making himself sick with revulsion.

Child abuse was an evil aspect in the extreme of humankind that he always knew was a solid base of hurt, sin and crime against the innocents in the world. He wiped those scenes out of his mind as he wiped the tears that he could not shed from the eyes he did not have.

Then he could see many rooms with naked and scantily dressed women. Nothing erotic or pleasing was seen by his shocked vision. He looked with apprehension at the scenes below and around him.

There were women who had been abused as children by their fathers, parental friends or others they thought that they could depend on. They had learned the false belief that giving their bodies would return them love and admiration from people who told them that it was alright to do what they had been told to do. Sometimes their bodies had been sold to the friends of fathers in return for drugs, money or a perverted gratification.

"Can you see where this is going?" The guide asked. "The women you used thought that your words and actions were genuine and they gave their bodies to you. You took them and then abandoned them. Is that use or abuse, Adam?

"You didn't break the law but you broke hearts and robbed those ladies of their self respect and pride. You were a prick in both senses of the word."

Feeling embarrassed and ashamed, Adam considered the high costs, to others, of his zeniths in terms of the nadirs he had provoked in his partners.

The scene kept changing like a rolling slide show.

He witnessed other abuses including the demands that sexual acts were performed for friends which would be watched and filmed for future use or added to porn sites on the internet.

There were young girls who had been forced into prostitution and drug abuse by men who wanted sex and profits from one source. But there were so many sources.

He saw women who were slaves. Trapped in homes to provide services of every nature and their only pay was being allowed to live and to maintain the preservation of their dismal lives.

Then a multitude of rapes of both men and women were happening. There was the spilling of blood and murders of horrific natures.

"Enough." Adam screamed at the horror.

"Where do the scales of abuse start and end, Adam? We will move on."

A door seemed to close on this scene as another opened.

Black and Blue

In the next room a man was shouting vile names at a terrified woman. He was slavering at the mouth. His anger was as intense as her fear. Then he slapped her and threw her to the ground. Adam could do nothing but felt dread and alarm. She laid on the ground bleeding from her nose. He kicked her in the stomach and laughed.

She spluttered words through her tears. "All I did was spill your beer. I am sorry." He kicked her again. "So maybe you will learn to be more careful, next time, you slut." He slurred.

The battered woman wanted to run, she wanted to be free of this tyrant, but she had nowhere to go. Her choices were staying with him or being homeless. This was part of his armoury. He could punch her, slap her and strangle her without fear because she thought she was dependant on him for her existence. If she escaped he would find her and inflict more beatings to punish her. She was stuck in this domestic cage fight. She was a spider in an enamel bath that scurried around looking for a wall to climb before she was squashed.

She was just one of so many. There was so much pain to witness and feel vicariously. So many bruises and broken limbs. So much screaming.

And to follow on in this menu of pain, Adam saw children bullying other children face to face, fist to face or by text or social media messages that eroded any self belief they had, even to the point of self-harm or suicide.

Yet even greatly diluted to an insult or a sarcastic word, those failings of mankind hurt to the extreme.

If, in his non physical state, he could have intervened then he would have. "Can you go there and make it stop as you did with Father Hugh?" Adam pleaded with his guide.

"I cannot. Abuse is very, very abundant in the world." The guide declares. "Although you know that, you can do little to stop it because it is outside your life. Once you were nearly a victim of abuse. You know how it feels. Become a champion for the abused men, women and children in the world.

Then the guide gave an instruction that Adam felt he had to obey.

"Do something when you get back to banish the suffering that you have just seen."

The door closed and yet another opened to the sound of Adam groaning.

Hurting Feelings

In that other place a man was trying to persuade his wife to dress in rubber underwear. She resisted with every defence she had. "It will put you in the mood for sex, darling." He wanted to take photographs that would end up on the internet.

"I do not want to dress up in that stuff and I will never be in the mood for sex with you ever again." She pleaded.

"If you can't be a proper wife then I will divorce you."

She was threatened with the economical ruin she would face without his financial support. "The children will starve." He panicked her with his words and she started to put on the latex pants he had given her. She would rather do what she hated than have her children face problems with their education and the false face of family life. She seemed to have no choice but to go along with him.

"Emotional abuse has many costumes." The guide told Adam.

There were men who were jealous of other men because they had pretty ladies in their lives. So they told them they were ugly, useless in bed and hopeless partners to have in order to smash their self belief like a cowboy breaking in a stallion that is a beautiful beast that had too much strength to be controlled unless dispirited and weakened.

And there were mind the games that unbalanced the ability to think clearly and attempted to imply madness in a partner. If somebody is called dim-witted for long enough they, unless they escape, will start to believe it is true.

And Adam could see mothers and fathers telling their children that they were stupid and lazy. Slapping and sobbing were the background noises in their lives.

If he had a body then he would have been vomiting from horror and shame.

He felt himself squirming with revulsion at these so called human beings, members of his own species who behaved in such a way that

54

is unknown to other creatures. They took pleasure and satisfaction from being heinous monsters who could only inflict physical and mental cruelty for reasons that Adam could not even begin to understand.

"There are things that hurt as much as a punch, Adam. Let's go."

Sticks and Stones

Suddenly, Adam was floating around the scenes where he had intimidated others for no reason other than for the outbursts a child makes when deprived of a packet of sweets on a supermarket shelf.

In hindsight and regret he was not sure what benefits could be derived from anger. The shouting, threatening and actions only caused problems galore. Yet those outbursts seemed to be uncontrollable and they released the pent up feelings of frustration at not getting what he wanted.

Even silent rage served little purpose, he thought. In the past it had hurt his career, his relationships and him.

He could see that from his invisible perch.

He could feel the pain and hurt that bad words had caused.

He condemned the gross exaggerations of the truth that stretched so much that they snapped and hurt the people who should be joined.

"Miserable cow." He heard a man shouting at a woman who was normally as happy as a cheery woman should have been.

"Slimy, foul mouthed bastard" she replied. Both of them so enraged at something trivial that grew to be monumental under the microscope of defence, one of the unmentioned parts of the fight or flight response.

The guide explained. "People fight off threats or they run away. But they can also freeze like a rabbit in headlights or defend when they wrap themselves into balls with their arms protecting themselves with an easily bruised coat of armour.

"There is physical hurt, emotional pain and self harm following an angry outburst. Nobody has ever won and everybody loses something.

"Partners run away having lost trust and love. It is virtually impossible to mend whatever happened."

Adam could see that. The misery he caused himself and others because he was unable to keep his feelings to himself and his mouth shut. And he was also hurt when he was the recipient of the vile rage of other men and women.

"You can see how much your anger has cost you," the Guide said, "and what happiness you could have found if you had counted to ten in your mind to allow yourself to decide the outcome you wished for. The scared base animal part of you took over and your contentment paid the price. Ask yourself, in the future, will my words lead to peace or to hostility? You are a man who likes to be liked but you are also a man armed with more weapons than the scorpion that stung you. Like him you grabbed others with spiky verbal pincers and stung with venom."

Sticks and stones will break my bones but words will always hurt me more. The thought was echoing around his mind.

He knew and he thought he always knew that words had the same effect as physical violence.

He realised how tears trickling down a person's face were the same as the flow of blood. A bruise to the body is the same as a black eye to the mind and emotions.

The guide interrupted his thoughts. "Any anger that is out of control leads to uncontrollable abuse. You have seen that in the other rooms you visited."

"What can I do?" He asked. "I cannot punish the men and women enough to stop abuse in the whole world. It needs something from a miraculous source to intervene and put an end to it."

"I will show you later but for now you can start with the abuse that you do to your body. Come with me."

Adam felt that he was being abused by the sights and sounds he had seen. He was in no mood for more.

Couch Potato

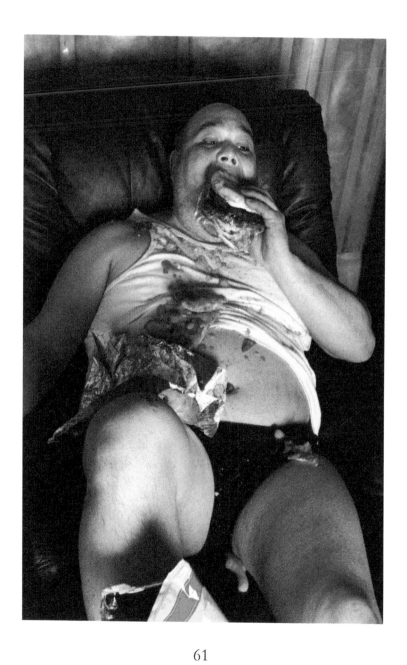

Still in shock at what he had seen, Adam entered what he recognised as the lounge in his house and there, slouched in his chair was a fat man eating burgers and fries. There was a glass of brandy at hand that came from a bottle that was nearly empty.

The only sounds he heard came from the blaring volume of the television serving up huge portions of nonsense and garbage. This was punctuated by loud belching and farting noises accompanied by raucous laughter.

It was not Adam sitting there, he was relieved to see.

The guide started to talk.

"This is an extreme representation of what you do. You gorged yourself with things that gave you pleasure, or the allusion of it.

"Life is not like watching television waiting to be entertained and complaining when you are not. People have to do something to bring sparkle into existence or they turn into mindless sponges that consume rubbish.

"Short term satisfaction, even at the price of long term harm, seems to be a driving force. A lot of your life has been waiting for things like sexual partners, jobs, money and so on without doing anything to gain or retain them or to earn their good feelings or even to deserve them."

Adam felt reprimanded for a life style that he could not easily admit to. He made excuses which were heartfelt and explained that he have been shown things for which he will find answers.

"But you have spent a lot of your life watching rather than doing. Find work that satisfies you, your employees, your employers and their customers. Even politicians have forgotten that their voters are their customers who they once pledged to serve.

"Find your sexual relief in a sharing, love filled relationship with somebody whom you respect and place as equal in your existence. Believe me; it is better because affection is the extra dimension that has been missing from your life. It is simple. Stop watching and start doing. Stop fornicating and start caring for the people you engage with."

If he could have let tears flow without his body then, once again it would have happened.

"On this note, respect your body, the transporter of your soul. If you had an expensive sports car you would have it serviced, valeted and you would have so much pride in it. You would have the engine looked at, checked the tyre pressures and you would have kept it like new."

He wondered where this was going.

"Your body has important parts that have to be kept in working order. They need your attention and admiration. Yet you smoke which clogs your lungs, drink too much and that hurts your liver. Both things damage the functioning of your heart and brain. Do you like the idea of a big lump of sculpted metal and plastic called a car to the person who would drive it if you had one?"

She paused.

"The body, your body, is there for the purpose of allowing you to live. Without it you would have no thoughts, no feelings, no happiness and no life. Do you want to end up like the guy on the couch, feeding laziness with food and lubricating it with brandy?

"And still on the subject of abuse, let us look at your alcohol consumption."

"Here I go again." He thought. "Back into the pit of remorse and castigation."

Getting Smashed

Adam was in a bar. He watched drunks drink to excess until they fell over. Like the chubby man they farted, belched and told sick jokes based on sex and racism.

The guide asked a rhetorical question. "Why is it that strong drinks are called 'eau de vie' when they can often be the cause of death?"

He admitted that he had sometimes drunk too much in his life. Again for his pleasure and an escape into a fantasy world, unlike the one he was in, where he could stagger and stumble without fear.

So different to this void he was in, where the demons that had haunted him could not be drunk away with the contents of a distillery.

Of course, anger could come from alcohol. Sometimes it relaxes but sometimes it aggravated and led to loss of control over the body and the mind. He was so aware of that.

To his embarrassment he was able to observe the times when the mostly sensible man, yet alone him, became an absolute idiot.

Adam was presented with an egg box with six eggs in it.

"Choose an egg." the guide told him.

He picked one and took it from the box. It hatched and a sweet yellow baby chicken emerged. It ran around chirping and assumed Adam was its parent and followed him looking for guidance and food.

"That is how we would like it. Take another."

He selected a second egg, it cracked and a tortoise made its way into the world. It had a shell that shone in the light. It had a nature that allowed it to hide from the world in its shell when it wanted so he was unable to see it at that moment.

"And one more."

This hatched and a venomous brown snake slithered out, raised itself to strike and stared at him. A kestrel appeared from the sky and picked it up to consume its catch.

"Drinking can produce human behaviours like those eggs picked at random. Some people become cuddly and warm. Others have hard shells that make them oblivious to what is going on around them.

"Then there are those that produce something venomous and threatening until it meets a bad end."

He could not help but wonder what the other three eggs contained. Perhaps children, perhaps tape worms, maybe dragons. Who knows?

"Alcohol is the catalyst that brings about change. Unless you know how you will hatch under the influence of booze you should stay away from it. If you do know how you will be, drink or reject it accordingly.

"And people can be a concoction of the three, sometimes a warm and lovely creature and sometimes a cold poisonous monster to be avoided at all costs."

The guide's words struck a chord with Adam. He had been all three of the creatures that hatched. He had been smooth and charming over a drink with a new girlfriend. Then sometimes hidden away when feelings became a handicap to his need for unconditional sex and then, very poisonous when drunk to excess and he felt under physical or emotional threat.

The thing that struck him hardest was the idea that a catalyst makes permanent change. He guessed the drunken guys he was witnessing had become that way eternally.

Adam, again wanting to run away, requested that they moved on to a different location or ideally returned to his old world.

Lost in the Old World

Lost in a forest, among trees that shuddered as if being besieged by a strong wind, Adam wondered where he was for the next nightmare.

Looking closer, he saw an impenetrable crowd of people resembling banks of trees.

They swayed and cleared every so often to give an impression of a way through.

When he got closer they were visible as individuals.

To his great surprise he could see his parents, grandparents and other relatives. Those people whose genes were in him. He had heard that when a person died they are greeted by their ancestors. This was a bad sign, he thought. Had he really died and floated into the afterlife? The guide must have been an assistant to St Peter because the judgement book had been thrown at him in a very heavy handed way and it had left huge bruises.

He looked for the welcoming smiles on their faces upon his arrival. But there was nothing but shame on their faces. No sense of pride. No satisfaction in the way he had lived with the life they had given him and then shared their love with.

"Who cares? They are old or dead anyway. Screw you." He mumbled to himself.

Then he started to shout. "You are the causes of my misery in life. Mother, you did not protect me from the priest. Father you did not give me as much pocket money as my friend got. You, my grandfathers, should have worked harder to build businesses that I could inherit and not have to work so hard myself. It is all of you I blame. It serves you right for being lonely and depressed now. You should have thought about the future."

His thoughts were beyond his control. Why was he so malevolent in his thinking about the people who cared for him as a child, adolescent and young adult? Why was he mentally throwing up this part digested vomit?

70

He wondered what truths the guide would bombard him with now.

She began. "What is hurting you is not the way your kin think or thought about you but, the projection of your opinions about yourself that have been placed on the people who you feel you have disappointed. That is part of your healing process that you have undertaken. I would worry more if those feelings had no affect on you at all. It is an old saying that people feel better after being sick and removing the poisons they had in their systems."

He needed to rush away yet again as if racing from his shame. Adam was running quickly through the woodland of people. Their arms and fingers were slapping his face like they would if they were branches.

It hurt. "Serves me right, I guess." He muttered to himself. "Anyway the old have had their lives."

Old and Frail

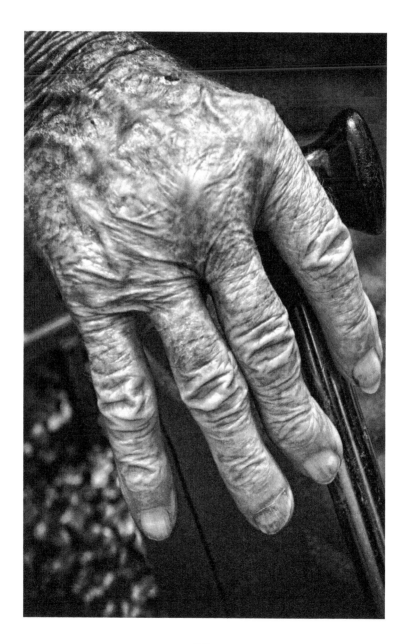

Adam was floating, as a free man, as if he was on a balloon away from the oppressive world he had been in. He had finally escaped.

Suddenly the balloon ripped open.

He plummeted to the ground, air rushing past him and fear growing larger with the perspective of his life about to crash into the earth.

Time froze for a moment or for an eternity.

Like a teacher from a Dickens book, the guide rose into an enormous entity and started to lecture Adam as if he had committed the most heinous crime.

"After all you have seen, after everything that was wrong in your life and in the world that has been presented to you, all that remains is the echo of your selfishness.

"Your forebears, grandparents and your parents are seen by you as the deliverers of the package of genes that you have. They had their lives and produced what would become you, the one and only thing that matters to you.

"Shame on you. You wanted to resolve your problems. You wanted to see why you were like you were. You are still as you were unless you get the idea that you share the world rather than own it.

"Money, women's' privates, power, booze and self satisfaction were, and still seem to be, your life."

As he hit the ground the breath and life were expelled from his body.

He was broken. He laid there crushed. His rant at his ancestors was the final straw that was breaking his camel's back. He needed to heal. He needed to change not just in words but in attitude, mind, body and soul.

That was the moment of transformation from what he had been, to what he would become. The blinding light of reality came on in his mind, soul and spirit.

He watched the sick, the old, the depressed and the confused crying from pain. This was the hurt from loneliness because their families had stopped contacting or visiting them.

They sat, alone, their spouses having died and left them with nothing but memories. The love they gave their children had been withheld from them because their offspring had other, more interesting, things to do. Or so they thought.

It could have been the result of bewilderment caused by dementia. Their kin had lost patience with the repetition or the incontinence and found avoidance a better way to cope than offering help and support.

Their aged, wrinkled fingers reached out to touch something that was no longer there, the love they once had has now been withdrawn.

They were like prisoners in solitary confinement waiting on death row. They were unable to talk to others. Their frail limbs were incapable of taking them out of their rooms.

Old people seem to be a burden only to the people who do not want to carry them. Those who help and return the love that their relatives, friends or acquaintances gave feel no load upon them.

Adam offered his fingers, his hand, his help and support to those broken people who had only committed the crime of growing old.

With difficulty at first he asked about their lives and their experiences. Then, without effort Adam listened, happy to hear the stories, humble to offer companionship and love that comes from sharing the tales, the emotions and the joy that is given unconditionally both ways.

Their life stories were like listening to a talking book. They explained what life was like in a history lesson complete with the graphic depictions of their times that are missed by somebody who did not live through wars, disease and poverty.

Adam was fascinated, enthralled and overjoyed at what he was hearing, not at the bad experiences that they endured but at their joy in finding an audience that listened.

"That is what needed to happen." Adam's guide smiled.

She had now taken on the shape of a naked nymph Adam noticed for the first time.

"I just wanted to see how you would react when you saw another naked woman." Her ironic sarcasm was not missed by Adam.

She smiled at him with that look of tenderness that a mother gives to her babies.

He had the feeling that she would go soon as she crouched in the position of a bird, or angel or a sprite about to take flight.

The Battle of the Soul

A very sweet voice was then talking to him. She sounded like his grandmother who he loved so very much. It had replaced that other one of his helper who had guided and chided him through this journey to this point that seemed to be the finale.

"The soul is about moral sense; the body is a selfish vehicle for the maintenance of life. The body looks for pleasure and dominance of other life forms including humans. It is as if the soul is sometimes like the primeval driver of a car that is out of control swerving, colliding and crashing.

"The battle in people is between the body's biological and chemical drives against the morality that the soul wishes to ensure a happy and fulfilling life for all.

"The soul wants to moderate but it sometimes gets pushed away. It can only try to influence good behaviour but it can be overruled by its lack of physical strength. It is a battle between the physical and the spiritual natures. It is the real essence of good versus evil on the planet.

"Evil is not something that comes from an outside source like the devil, it is the diminishing of the sense of integrity with which we are born. It is the sense of sharing that we get when we suckle. We need to take milk from our mothers and in return we give them back joy at having created and nurtured life.

"Wars are fought by people who want to persuade others that it is moral to kill and to die for a cause that is based on the selfishness, greed and power of dictators, despots and politicians.

"Reduce that universal idea to the individual and you will see that your bodily needs and lust have been winning against the benevolence of your soul and have smothered wellbeing and love.

"The body is about the Self, the soul is about sharing. The two need to work in harmony rather than fighting a war. Your soul had separated from your body in the sweat lodge in order for you to make the changes you asked for at the beginning.

"You made your personal prayer asking for the resolution of all your problems. The way was made for you to do that very thing.

"Learn to care and share in order to bring order to your life."

Adam absorbed the words as if they were the magic potion he had sought, the elixir of life in a verbal form.

"So who are you?" Adam asked. "Are you really my gran or are you God or an angel?"

"I am none of those but I am speaking with a tone of voice that you will take heed of. I am your thinking mind, the connection between your physical body and your soul. It is the part of you that makes change possible. In other words I am your conscience. You need to learn how to share to give joy and pleasure to all life and in return they will share that with you."

Adam asked, "Is the soul you are talking about the bit of me that goes on after I die, if I am not dead already?"

The reply from a voice, that was fading, combined his intention and objective into something concrete and genuine.

"After death the most complete souls go higher. It is like a hierarchy of virtue. That is why when children die their souls float brightly because they are uncorrupted.

"We shall meet again, Adam, if you want help. Just ask and you will find answers. The voice you hear will be yours because I am a part of you and I will assist you to make the correct choices in your life. The voice you will hear is inside your head, not in a crazy way but in thoughts of benevolence."

She disappeared from his eyes and ears. She had gone leaving Adam to return to his recognisable world.

The Eve of Light

Adam woke up from his dream, journey or nightmare. He did not know what it had been.

His head was buzzing with the memories of his expedition into his mind and soul.

He seemed to be weak as if the episode had been physical as well as mental. Getting to his feet he looked around. It was still night time, but the full moon gave a gentle muted light.

"Are you alright mate? You was out like a light for about ten minutes." A male human voice with a heavy London accent guided him back to land like an air traffic controller.

Ten minutes? It seemed like weeks.

The woman he had noticed from the beginning who had seemed remote was sat on the ground nearby. She was holding her head as if she had seen the Devil. Like Adam, she was still naked. He remembered her from when they had all met up for the preliminary small talk and an introduction to what they were to do in the sweat lodge.

She had the same look of confused realisation that he must have been wearing.

Other people were wandering around looking for their clothes and strolling back to the farm house where they had met.

At the same point Adam and the girl both became aware that they were naked and making silly excuses, they both moved off to recover their clothes. She had been undressed but, for the first time in his life Adam felt sympathy for the plight of a woman's nakedness in front of a stranger. Rather than lusting at this beautiful sight he rejected any feelings of voyeurism.

After they had both dressed they walked back together in silence for a drink of water.

The others were sitting around in the big farm kitchen talking about their experiences. None of them seemed to have been where Adam had been.

He went to bed and slept, dream free, until morning broke.

After breakfast, as if they were drawn together, both of them walked into the forest at the back of the farm and started chatting.

They started to talk in low and slow tones, sharing their episodes in the weird location that could not be defined as it had only existed in their own minds or souls.

"I am worried." She said. "I think somebody had spiked my drink with LSD or something. I had some strange experiences, Adam. It is Adam? "She asked."Corny, isn't it? My name is Eve." She laughed.

"I had the some uncanny thoughts as well." He reassured her. "And I had taken my own water in a bottle so nobody had spiked my drinks. What happened to you?"

She started to talk about her own journey. Although at first she was embarrassed, after support from him, she talked openly about her meetings with guides and monsters and how she had witnessed herself being a horrible and selfish person to her boyfriends, bosses and family. Adam listened attentively and the look on his face told her that he had shared some of the same events.

Then they talked about everything and nothing for hours to give each other a perspective on how they got to their stages in life. Perhaps for the first time, both of them were exploring mental and emotional processes rather than the body shape and what it offered sexually.

From what she said, her journey had been similar to his and her mission to discover the values that she should apply for her happiness and for the mutual joy of others had been full of the experiences that had bared her soul to her.

What they agreed was that the sweat lodge was a simple wooden frame, naked to the world before it had been clothed with its cover of canvas, twigs and earth like a warm womb for them to be reborn in.

It was an analogy for what the start of their adventures had been.

In contrast, the participants were stripped and ready for the entry into a new world like being born backwards. They had been full of bad attitudes and behaviours that boiled away to leave a clean residue that they could recognise now as their metaphorical souls that can exist with their minds and bodies without causing harm to others.

They both had felt that they had been placed in a symbolic womb that represented the continuing circle in that setting of destruction and construction.

The conclusion was that sharing without expecting anything is the key that frees the soul.

What they found difficult was figuring the mechanism for their change. Had it really been a meeting with a spirit guide or an opening of the hidden doors in their minds that had been brought about by the intensity of the heat and the ritualistic nature of the whole event?

Or had they been driven to hallucinate something by the intensity of the moment?

Did it matter? The truth and realisation that resulted was the key to reviewing their attitudes and behaviours.

And so they both agreed that it had been a life changing experience and that they had learnt a new way to live.

Caring and Sharing

As they walked further towards the edge of the forest Adam took in the view in front of him.

He could see green. Not just green but the infinite shades that make up grasses, leaves, moss and light and shadow. He felt like a landscape painter choosing colours from his pallet. Adding tones, shades and textures, this was the first time he had seen what there is to be seen.

Smells were beautiful. The subtle earthy essence of truffles deep in the ground. The air of pastures that creatures lived in and fed on and the long lingering aftertastes of perfection. The fragrance from varieties of flowers, the aroma of the perfume Eve was wearing, the bouquets of fine wines. Everything was potent and full of magnificence.

Adam heard music that spanned every genre from pop to classical, from folk to jazz, from blues to opera. This was music stored in his mind that he could access by thought alone.

He was able to feel in a sensitive way. He remembered the fur of a kitten, the skin of a person he had loved, the textures of materials from silk to earth.

This was being alive. To sense the world as it is. A library of experiences that we need to read from A to Z rather than cherry pick the bits that appeal to us and reject the rest without desire or enthusiasm because we have no understanding.

A collection of never ending feelings and emotions of care for all other people, the creatures of the planet, the plants that grow on it and the very base of all life...the earth.

Unconditional love where we can give without expectation. Not desiring a return on our outlay. Just sensing the warmth that we give is pleasure enough.

He realised that sharing with all forms of life is more important than getting things and guarding them for personal satisfaction.

Sharing is giving food to the birds in a garden and receiving the joy of watching them. They will never say "thank you" in words but the life that is sustained gives an enormous enjoyment to the universal pleasure of the world.

Giving an old coat or a sweater to somebody who is poor and cold will cost nothing but will give a dividend beyond measure to the recipient. It might be the stimulus that allows him or her to get up and seek what they want from life rather than from a bottle or a needle.

He had a sense that his guide was watching even from the vantage point that was in his own head. He was straining to do what is right for all and hoped to bring a smile to her face.

Possibly she had arranged for him to meet somebody for whom he had respect. A woman who was more than just a receptacle for his passion, a receiver of his penis. Somebody with whom he could share love.

He agreed with Eve that they would meet up on the following weekend at a cabin on the coast that belonged to her parents.

She gave him the address and Adam left looking forward to the following Saturday.

No sexual advances were made by either of them. A kiss on the cheek was their token of companionship as they said goodbye and drove away to their different destinations.

Dreamtime

Both of them had vivid dreams that would take them to their own memories of their journeys into their mental realms that stayed invisible when awake.

Adam watched wolves catching deer. He was worried that violence had not been eliminated from his dream world but then he saw the wolves working as a team. They only hunted when they were hungry never for fun. The food they caught was shared with the whole pack with no fighting or squabbling. The pups were a priority being the next generation.

Then he had dreams of being around nice, friendly people who derived their pleasure from looking at nature, helping others whether they were human or other creatures and, basically helping others to live a life that shared satisfaction.

The dream that stayed most strong in his head was the fusion of the ban-the-bomb symbol with a heart of love mixed with a dove of peace. They moved around, formed into a pill which Adam ate.

Banning war, hatred and weapons combined with love and universal peace should be the dream and ambition of all mankind, he thought when he awoke.

"I have become a New Age freak." He thought over his breakfast on the Saturday morning of his visit to see Eve.

The idea of meeting her again brought a flicker of delight to his mind. Not just because she had a beautiful face and an exquisite body but because their minds seemed to share a frequency of compatibility.

It Did Not Stop There

Adam arrived on the Saturday morning, but nobody was in the house. Nobody answered the door.

Wondering where Eve was he walked to the empty beach he could see nearby. The weather was warm but not hot enough to fill the seashore with sun-seekers. There was nobody there.

With a feeling of disappointment at her absence he walked along the coast in search of her.

Still no Eve in sight but he turned his view inland at the sandy dunes where he saw her meditating. She was naked and beautiful and looked so much at peace. She was oblivious to the world.

Without thoughts of desire Adam stripped naked, thanking his lucky stars that the beach was empty, and joined her. After all they had seen each other in their birthday suits the weekend before so it was not such a strange thing to do. Anyway, this was sharing of a state rather than a build up to sex as it would have been in their pasts.

He sat, cross legged beside her and closed his eyes. Concentrating on his slow breathing he felt at ease. He was both alone and in the company of somebody who was different to all the women who had gone before. He became aware of the musky smell of the woman next to him. There had been no verbal or physical communication but there had been no need of such.

He knew that his spirit guide was close by; he could feel her presence but had no sight nor sound of her. His heart was beating to the rhythm of the waves lapping on the shore. He was at peace with this new world.

Then he felt a hand take his and he opened his eyes to see Eve smiling.

"I knew that you would know where to find me and that you would know what to do." She leaned over and they shared their first kiss.

They had met as naked bodies that needed to be repaired and now they had met as naked souls that had been healed and reborn.

92

Epilogue

Adam described his experience as being like a mental boil bursting in his head that released the pus and poison of a lifetime of ruthlessness and selfishness and that he was cleaned to the point where new life could grow to replace the rot.

With Eve, they discussed the experiences they had shared but as separate people. They wondered if they had undergone 'out-of-body' experiences caused by the heat and the effects on their bodies.

But they both agreed that those events resulted in both of them seeing the entrance to Heaven and knowing that they had each seen their personal Hells.

They met afterwards many times and shared love in their beds rather than lust. Their courtship was based on building love rather than on sex and that felt so much better than in their old lives.

They searched for the enjoyment of life and that involved getting to know other people, relatives and friends for their qualities rather than what they could do for them. Their personal pleasure came in the wake of the joys they gave.

Adam's working life changed as he helped employees to grow and develop skills to succeed. It was like watering plants in a drought. They grew and shone with shared results.

Together they used their sharp minds to start charities that helped the poor and starving in their own country as well as abroad.

Above all, Adam and Eve found the delights of life with each other. The love they share and which grows daily is theirs, the happiness that they have is given to others to bring light into their lives.

As a result of their experiences they put their heads together and wrote the following guide to contentment and happiness so that they could share what they had found in their hearts, souls and minds as a contribution to building for others what their guides had made possible for them.

CONTENTMENT
by Adam and Eve Rice

The following is a text written by us after our experiences in the sweat lodge.

The fundamental gift is that of sharing and the words are brought to you with an open heart and a wish that they will provide the readers with an insight into making positive changes to their lives.

It is written as a list of choices rather than as a 'must do' instruction. Please choose whatever you wish from the contents.

And above all, we wish you a satisfying and happy life

With best regards

Adam and Eve

Misery

Contentment is not the fulfilment of what you want, but the realization of how much you already have.
Anon.

There are two causes of misery, having things that you do not want and not having things that you do want.

If you want a happy life, and most of us do, hopefully these words will show you how to stop making it unhappy. The aim is to help you to find real contentment in your life.

This text contains lots of suggestions for the reader to look at. They are like items on a menu. You can pick and choose rather than consume them all. You can always come back for more. They will apply to you when they are relevant to your needs.

The purpose of the words that follow is to share the means to find contentment for you. As you will see later, sharing is an important component in your recipe for creating a better life.

You will not be told what to do. Orders do not lead to contentment. In fact giving and receiving them causes problems.

The text is short and to the point, deliberately. We could waffle on to fill pages but the need to find contentment is in the 'here and now' rather than in a lengthy study course that will take unnecessary time to finish.

Please read through the points that follow at your own pace but do your best to make any changes that you feel will help you.

Contentment is available wherever you live, however much money you have, or do not have, and with who-ever you share your life with or would like to.

This is not a book full of instructions that must be obeyed. Instead it is a straightforward guide that is full of helpful tips for achieving contentment.

The changes you will make may seem unusual at first but really they are not that difficult. The end result is always worth the effort. If you do not perfectly match the recipe then you will still end up with something worthy and satisfying.

The ingredients that you will need are listed as we move on. They come as different flavours and quantities. But unlike a food recipe too much or too little will not spoil the outcome but making the effort to use the components will achieve a better outcome for your life.

Contentment

What is contentment?

The answer is never a simple one. It does not come as a yes or no, or right and wrong. It is an amalgam of lots of different elements, like in a recipe for fine food.

Contentment seems to be described in emotional terms rather than financial ones.

Being contented is having peace of mind, feeling good about your life and your surroundings.

It is also about how you are at this moment in time.

Savour the Moment

You are living now and you will live in the future. The past has gone, it cannot be changed. There are no options for 'replay'.

If you are searching for contentment then it will arrive when you want it to or, even better, now.

If it will happen tomorrow, next week, next month or next year it follows that you are unhappy now. Let us think of today as the beginning of the change that is taking place.

That means that you can view today differently. There is an old saying that states that 'a long journey starts with a small step'. Why assume your change is a long journey? It can be instantaneous. You are dealing with your emotional wellbeing rather than with a physical distance.

Concentrate on the things you can change rather than those you cannot. Newspaper headlines are based on bad and sad news, the items that sell newspapers rather those that inform the reader of what is good in the world.

If the summer is hot then you are told we are experiencing a heatwave and people will die. If it is cold then we will die from illnesses brought about by germs attacking us. If it is raining then we will worry about flooding.

Enjoy these changes in the weather and take precautions if it is going to be severe and dangerous. It does not effect many people but it worries us enough to watch the news and buy newspapers.

Headlines, in a way, are what mislead you because bad news is a headline, and gradual improvement is not. ***Bill Gates***

Learn to savour the moment. If your past is sad then see a great future growing from today. The past is finished. The future starts with every moment that happens from now. It is, and will be, different if you make it so.

If you are only aware of the 'bad headlines' in your life then, together we will turn the page to find the good news.

Dismiss those things that have made you unhappy, they are yesterday's news. Begin your better life...now.

Who Controls You?

There is a very definite relationship between control and contentment. This is not one sided. We can feel controlled by other people, rules and by money. Then there are those people who seem to have control but may fear that they will lose it.

Part of control is restraint. The prevention of something or somebody's behaviour is at the heart of the matter. If you control somebody then you will upset them and likewise if you are controlled then you cannot do what you would like to do.

Break the chains that bind you and keep you from enjoying your life.

What we need is **balance** so we are not over controlled and so we do not control things or events to excess.

Sometimes you will be the person who wants to control and the reaction you get is opposite to the one intended. If you tell jokes all the time then rather than getting laughs you will alienate your fellows. Sharing jokes is fine when you are telling them in the right context and as long as you listen to the others you will be welcomed.

The same applies to conversations. Listening and sharing is the most important thing to do.

Part of contentment is having others around you who are also contented in your company. If you hog conversations or lecture rather than share your chat then you will push people away. There is a wonderful saying that expresses it beautifully; 'You have two ears and one mouth, use them in those proportions.'

If you make that a rule then the end result is usually 50/50 but you will be seen as a person who others can have a talk with.

Remember the Simon and Garfunkel song, "The Sound of Silence":
People talking without speaking,
People hearing without listening.

Some people will only talk about themselves and anything you say will be returned to you in terms of their experiences without wanting to hear what you have to say. They need to learn how to listen. If you are like that, then you need to listen and show interest in what others are saying.

Feel like a member of a modern species. In our primeval history life was about hunting, cooking, sex for breeding and sleep.

Now we have complex language that can express emotions. We can see where an old life such as a stag can bring about discontent. The dominant animal has to fight to retain his females that he services for his short term pleasure and then he has to protect his place against his competition. His longer term contentment is always controlled by others.

Key Points

*Seek balance in your life. Avoid being negatively controlled and avoid controlling others.

*Control the amount of control that exists in your life either incoming or outgoing.

*Listen more than you talk. People will like you more.

Sharing and Helping

We live in a complex social world where we like to know where we fit in.

Sharing is not about giving something away that you lose. It is about gaining. It is a mutual exchange of anything from money, food, emotion and friendship.

Imagine opening a bottle of wine. If you drink it all then you might lose control and lose friends. If you share it then you will spread pleasure in a generous act. Sharing has huge benefits. Rather than wine, imagine you are sharing joy, happiness and contentment.

Another example is a pizza cut into slices. Would you eat the whole thing in front of hungry friends? No, you would offer slices to them and they would be distributed evenly. All of you would be happy.

Money

Bill Gates has made an absolute fortune and he has shared much of it with others by way of foundations and charity gifts. Is he content? You bet.

There are huge companies that have a profit sharing system with employees. This leads to a higher level of job performance and satisfaction.

What is not being suggested is that you share your money unless you can afford to but there are some universal hints that giving and sharing will result in gaining a return. Perhaps that is emotional rather than financial but it offers contentment. Certainly happiness is enhanced by being as generous as possible when needed.

Feeding your pets and wild birds will never end in them saying 'thank you' when you share your money and time in buying food and putting it out but they will give you a sense of satisfaction because you have enriched their lives.

Love and Sex

Love making is a mutual pleasure because the sharing of bodies is satisfaction for both parties. Sex, however can be one sided. If one partner demands sex for their own relief then the other person is left feeling used. That emotion of being exploited will return to the user in different ways.

If love making cannot be a shared joy then it is necessary to find out why one of you is eating the whole pizza and drinking the whole bottle of wine.

Talk to each other but most importantly listen.

Time

Away from love making and sex, share time to share experiences. Find out what your partner and other people like doing. Even if what they want to do is contrary to what you like to do, the result you will get will far outweigh any discomfort you felt from giving happiness to somebody. If they like walking on a beach, join in, for example.

Things

Share vegetables with friends and neighbours from your garden if you have an excess. What you will receive will be a kind thought if nothing else.

Share your lunchtime sandwich with the birds in the park.

Stop worrying about the trivial things in life and allow yourself to enjoy the bigger joys of life.

Lonely people do not have others to share with but people who share are less likely to be lonely.

Key Points
*Sharing is a great way to gain happiness and friends. Two or more people in a joint enterprise make it so much easier.

*Love making is sharing whereas sex for one person's relief is hurtful to a relationship.

Scales of Contentment

There is a timescale for contentment.

Short term pleasure will leave you wanting more and more because you are feeling good in the present time and you want it to continue.

Long term contentment is when it is spread over your life. Perhaps it is not as intense as the short boost but it will be a goal to aim for as it lasts and lasts.

There are components of contentment which vary.

Perhaps laying in the garden in the sunshine. Maybe going for a walk, eating, meeting others. These cannot all be done at the same time but they will set the balance of contentment at an optimum level for you.

In short, be contented doing whatever you are doing without worrying that you are not doing something else. Live in the happy moments.

You always have choice. I have seen a 94 year old woman making sure she walked a small distance to keep her body moving. I also know a 92 year old woman who only moves around when she is on holiday. And finally another younger person who is happy to sit and watch the television and be waited on by her partner. These are three different facets of contentment. There are no rights and wrongs, no judgement. However there is a balance in the larger picture.

If you want to read a book or listen to music and it makes you happy, do it.

Allow things to happen in your life that satisfy you. Do what you feel like doing if it does no harm to others. There are no extra rules other than being honest with other people and to yourself.

It is your life after all, it does not belong to others.

Key Points

*Look for contentment now and in the future. It is your life so do what makes you and others happy as long as it does not makes others miserable.

Setting Your Mindset

Your mind is like a loyal dog. It will do what you train it to do. If you train it to scare people then that is what it will do.

If you believe a house is haunted then sooner or later you will see a ghost.

There was a Tommy Cooper joke that says he went to the doctor and said 'it hurts when I do that', so the doctor said ' well don't do that'. When you tell yourself that you are unhappy or miserable then you will feel that way. Stop doing it!

Believe in the idea that contentment is achievable and you will find contentment.

Belief in a good future brings it about.

There are some thinking traps that need to be disabled. The next section shows you how to do that.

Key Points

*You can train your mind to be positive and you can teach it to stop being miserable.

*Believe in your present and future wellbeing.

Training Your Mind

Our self-talk is full of traps. Most people have heard of the word 'affirmation', a positive phrase or suggestion aimed at changing the ways in which we think about ourselves. The most famous one is "Everyday, in every way, I am getting better and better."

However, very few people actually use positive affirmations. Most of us are very adept at using negative ones by accident! We develop and hold onto erroneous beliefs that distort and change our behaviours and attitudes.

Sadly, we are wonderful in reinforcing negatives by our thinking. When we make negative suggestions to ourselves then we run a huge risk of believing them.

Suggestions like the following need to be ruthlessly destroyed.

"I am unlucky," "I am ugly," "I am a loser" and "I will get fired because I am useless at my job."

There is a way to break the negativity of our self-talk. We use very positive techniques for changing our language, which in turn modify our thinking, emotions and reactions. These are based on eliminating negative words and conditions. We replace them with a language and thinking that contains beneficial intention and positive intent.

The rules and steps are simple and easy to remember.

Look at the sentence 'I will NOT feel unhappy (or not get angry/become anxious/get stressed, etc.) in my life (or in the car, at the restaurant, at work, on a date, etc.) This seems as if it will work.

However, within that short sentence there are three fundamental errors of thought that will bring about the opposite response. From working through this example, we see how to turn our goals into language that communicates the correct message to our minds.

1. 'I WILL' puts the hoped for solution into the future. The future is tomorrow, next week, next year, whatever. This tells us that whereas relief will be found, it is unlikely that it will help us now. Putting that hope into the future reinforces the problem that you currently have.

So the first rule and step is to place your problem into the past tense.

If it WAS a problem, then it follows that it has gone. Your mind gives you the unconscious positive suggestion, or affirmation, that you need. You put the solution into the present tense by using the words 'I' and 'NOW

The affirmation then becomes: 'I used to feel unhappy in my life (or whatever) BUT NOW, I feel peaceful, safe and relaxed.'

If you find that your mind tells you that your problem still exists, then argue with it! Repeat your affirmation over and over.

2. The second rule is to lose the small word 'NOT'.
Although we know what positive suggestions are, we fail to use them. Instead, anxiety sufferers use negative suggestions accidentally. These maintain the problem rather than giving a solution. When we are thinking about behaviours, our minds seem to be unable to recognise negatives. When we use the word 'NOT' we often create the opposite outcome to that which is desired. Let me give an example: 'Do NOT think of blue elephants!'

It is likely that you thought of blue elephants. It therefore follows that the sentence 'I will NOT feel unhappy in my life' is understood as 'I WILL feel unhappy in my life' because the instruction is contained after the word 'NOT' in the words 'feel unhappy in my life'. The

111

word 'not' has no effect in changing that instruction.

The blue elephant example told you, after the word 'NOT', to think of blue elephants.

So, use a sentence that affirms what you want to happen rather than using a negative in an attempt to negate the unwanted effect. To repeat, lose the word 'NOT' from your thoughts. In its place, state the result that you want in positive terms.

A quick note. Whereas the word 'not' is to be avoided in suggestions and self talk dialogue, it is permitted in negating things as in 'blue is not green'.

3. The third rule, and next step, is to omit any reference to the problem when you are used to putting it into the past and when you have stopped using the word 'not'.

The last part of the sentence is a reminder of the problem and it is emphasised. '...feel unhappy in my life.' It tells you to do what you want to avoid.

Never feed a problem by talking or thinking about it. Starve it to death. Make it an exile, something that used to cause upsets but which has now been eliminated.

Eliminate the problem and tell yourself what you want to happen. 'In my life (or in the car, at the restaurant, at work, on a date, etc.), I am calm, confident and in contented'.

Putting It Together:

1. Make your suggestions positive, current and relevant to the solution. Ignore the problem completely. It is something that you used to have, but now you are fine.

2. Avoid certain other words such as 'perhaps', 'ought', 'should', 'maybe', 'if', 'might', 'probably' and 'try'. These imply either failure or weakness.

3. Make your internal dialogue strong and assertive. Tell yourself what you want to be by telling yourself that what you once wanted in the future is how you actually are, NOW.

4. To summarise, model your suggestion on the following, "In my life I am calm, peaceful, contented and relaxed." Stop your language from telling you otherwise.
Can you now see why 'DON'T PANIC' is the WORST thing to say in a crisis? 'STAY CALM AND RELAXED' is so much better.

So for you, how about, "I used to feel unhappy and discontented BUT NOW I feel wonderful and happy in my life."

Key Points

*Eliminate negative thoughts by eliminating negative words in your internal dialogue.

*Make positive affirmations about how you want to feel but apply them to the 'here and now'.

Emotional Contentment

Emotional contentment is not based on the amount of money you spend, it is reliant on your emotional state.

It is about being happy with the way things are in your life or are becoming.

There are wealthy people who are content and there are wealthy people who are not. Similarly there are poor people who are happy and those who are not.

Remember what was said before. 'There are two causes of misery, having things that you do not want and not having things that you do want'.

The discontented wealthy people want to make more money and/or have more control over other people. Perhaps they worry about the financial crisis in the World or about signs of aging and buy the sometimes catastrophic results of cosmetic surgery.

Maybe they want to live in different parts of the world but their friends and family are more geographically fixed and so become remote. And so on. Have you ever wondered why so many pop stars and actors take to drugs and alcohol. A mansion in California can become a lonely place where the stars are surrounded by false friends.

The happy ones live within the natural processes of life and travel through time with dignity and acceptance of their fate. They can be reassured by their resources and feel secure enough not to require pleasures that have to be bought.

The same applies to the happy less well off who enrich their lives with friends and family. Rather than going to concerts or the theatre they can be happy with watching events on their television sets and sharing a meal and a joke with similar folk.

In England there was a 'celebrity' who was held in high esteem and was worth £11 million ($19 million). He was convicted of child abuse. In my head and in the heads of most people this made him totally worthless as a human. That is the true value of the man. I laugh as I wonder how he will spend all that money before he dies, probably in prison.

Compare him to a man I saw in Mumbai on a business trip that I was making. I had to take a bus between the International Terminal to the Domestic one. From this bus I saw the slum shacks at close quarters, some housing people and one housing about eight buffalo. These sheds, by Western standards, were horrible.

The inhabitants, however, looked relaxed, almost like tourists on holiday in the Mediterranean resorts, keeping out of the sun. They were happy with this way of life. I suppose they were in a community where all were equal, no snobbery, just sharing life.

A man stepped out of his shack and started to pee onto the dried earth. He had no signs of having money but he had a look of peace and contentment on his face, one that said he felt sorry for those of us on the bus hustling and bustling to make our pay cheques. An artist would have painted that look as a thing of beauty. He would have accepted a few rupees as a gift but he seemed happy without it. Money was not his goal. He just enjoyed his simple life with his family and friends.

Sadly, we value things by their cost and we value people by their assets. These are transient, hollow measures of worth. You have what you have, be grateful. When you are greedy you will be in that place where you want more for the sake of possessing it. That brings discontent.

Few are the rich people who do not want more money. They cannot reach the ceiling and they are unhappy with their wealth. Far better are the rich people who share their wealth for the benefit of others.

Getting back to the 'celebrity' child abuser for a moment, he was probably content that his perverted needs were satisfied without any consideration for the feelings of those he abused. His short-term selfish contentment has turned out to be the cause of his misery, now he is in jail. Sadly the hurt that his victims felt and feel will not go away with his conviction but they might feel some contentment that they helped to bring about justice and that they have, at last, been believed.

His reputation and respect were demolished in the moment of being found guilty. It is a shame that it did not apply to the other celebrities and politicians who used their money, power and influence to wreck lives before they died, but hopefully it will restrain others.

Key Points

*Contentment is an emotional thing that never depends of the amount of money that you have. It is free.

*Selfish contentment will blow up in your face. Share the joys of life with others.

No Man Is An Island

Lives can be like living on a desert island even when we are surrounded by fields, buildings or people. We can feel isolated wherever we are.

Even Robinson Crusoe was grateful to the company and help shared by Man Friday. At first they could not communicate because they spoke different languages. This problem took time to overcome, but in the end they had a good and strong relationship.

In your mind you could imagine living on a desert island and wondering what you would like to be there with you. Your island could appear to be in your relationships with the other person on a near but separate island. What could you do to build a bridge between the two?

On your island what would you need and what would you like to abandon? You would not need money because there would be nowhere to spend it.

Answering these questions can set you in a different frame of mind about what you would like to do with your life.

Contentment is not just a singular personal thing. It is built in a nest of contentment from others so you are sharing your peace of mind.

It is also feeling part of something but compare belonging to a gang that sells drugs to young teenagers with working for a charity that rescues drug users. Who would feel more contented when they are in bed and there is a knock on the door? This is related to feeling fulfilled in what you are doing.

Be contented doing what you are doing. Sitting in the garden shelling peas is boring to some but a joy for others.

Dream what you would like to be doing that would make you happy and then work towards that objective and it will happen. Moaning about what you do not have is destructive; planning a happy future is the start of a contented time.

Key Points

*Think about what you would need to feel really contented and then make that dream a reality by taking positive actions.

Anticipate Your Pleasure

If you want contentment look forward to it with your inner eyes, your imagination. Whatever we desire is available if we consider our needs without greed or harm to others.

This is not some sort of spiritual or new-age spell, it just seems to work because you set your mind to recognise people, things and events that will help you to achieve your goals.

We receive so much information that the mind has to ignore in order to sort the wheat from the chaff.

When we dream of our aims then it as if a door in that wall of rejection is left open for ideas and hints to gain access. The expression 'closed mind' fits this explanation well when it is joined to 'open minded'.

An open mind is receptive to new ideas and clues.

The first step is to loosely define what you would like to have in emotional terms. The concrete resources you need will follow on behind.

It goes a bit like this:

If you want a holiday in Florida imagine yourself and others on a beach in the sunshine enjoying the smells of the ocean, the feel of the sand, the sounds of the waves lapping on the shore, the taste of the food you will find there. Hold these sensory images in your mind and you will find coincidences that will help you to achieve that dream.

Keep it in those exiting images of the result. If you imagine the physical money you would need to pay for it, however, then your dream will bring no result apart from frustration at not getting it.

Money is a tool for trading and it does not exist in the fabric of the mind in terms of what it can buy. You have to see and feel the result you are looking for rather than the simple tool for buying it.

Dreams are always emotional and are a powerful force.

There is a quote allegedly by Goethe that says:

"Until one is committed, there is hesitancy, the chance to draw back. Concerning all acts of initiative (and creation), there is one elementary truth, the ignorance of which kills countless ideas and splendid plans: that the moment one definitely commits oneself, then Providence moves too. All sorts of things occur to help one that would never otherwise have occurred. A whole stream of events issues from the decision, raising in one's favour all manner of unforeseen incidents and meetings and material assistance, which no man could have dreamed would have come his way. Whatever you can do, or dream you can do, begin it. Boldness has genius, power, and magic in it. Begin it now."

How this works is beyond logic but it seems to bring results about.

Key Points

*Use your imagination to conjure up the emotional results you desire.

*Allow the events and people that will help you to achieve your dreams to enter your life and thinking.

Inner Peace From Outside

Meditation is hard. Finding inner peace by using the traditional meditation methods takes a lot of effort. Rules have been established for body position and repetitive mantras. Like lots of esoteric knowledge it is too full of impediments to be easy or fast.

We will take a shortcut.

Think of contemplation instead. This is about looking at things and thinking about them. Not in a candle staring way but admiring things around you. Examples could be watching birds feeding in your garden or in a park. It could be watching a fishing float bobbing around in rippling water. It could be watching people in a non-scary way in a shopping mall while you sip a cup of coffee.

In fact think of contemplation as a form of daydreaming. Take inspiration from things around you and apply those thoughts to your situation that you want to improve.

Key Points

*A great way to enjoy your thoughts is to take peace from your surroundings and mix them.

*Contemplation is a fast way to find relaxation.

Those Who Surround You

Think of yourself as being in a small boat on the open seas.

With true contentment in yourself then the water around you is calm. If you are surrounded by discontented people then the water becomes choppy and you are feeling less secure and comfortable. If you upset other people then a storm breaks, the water becomes rough and threatens to sink you.

Think of your friends both current and past. Friendships are worth their weight in something more precious than gold.

There are ways to keep in touch with people. Letters, emails, postcards, seasonal greetings and, of course, the telephone. Rather than waiting for them to contact you, take the initiative today.

If you worry that they will not want to hear from you then you have postponed something that might be as heart-warming for them as it is for you. We are social creatures by nature. They need contact as much as you and perhaps they are worried that you do not want to hear from them. Be the initiator.

Key Points

*Surround yourself with friendly people.

*Keep in touch with your friends and family.

Using Social Media

Social media sometimes get a bad press. It is implied that the Internet connections inhibit 'real' friendships, they makes you isolated and so on. But if you are isolated, have no friends and have no contacts then you can get these from your social media pages.

After all they are so popular because lots of people use them. Life is not usually full of meeting strangers in the shopping mall with whom you can have a conversation. Places to meet people in 'real' life are fraught with the same dangers as the internet. There are sharks who want you for their own pleasure.

If you need contact with people or you wish to meet folk with similar interests then use social media.

However always be wary of people you meet either in a public place or on the Internet, but having said that, you can, if you are careful, find folk to share interests with.

Key Points

*Use social media if you find making face to face friends difficult.

*Be careful when contacting strangers. Some are not what they seem to be.

Things to Do

Allow happiness to happen. It is your life, not others.

Accept the benefits of doing something for others and yourself and you will receive the benefit yourself. In other words, if you want to go for a walk sell the ide to others by talking about seeing the ducks, smelling wild flowers, getting some exercise rather than talking about walking which has less appeal.

Go to a concert or art gallery where you might meet somebody who shares your interests.

Going to bars needs to be done with caution as you might meet somebody whose hobby is drinking or they are there because they need somebody to be sad with.

You could take an evening class in something that interests you. Others in the class will have similar interests to you by being there as well.

You can do things for charity. You will meet other people and you can feel useful to society. It also gives you something to occupy your spare time.

Key Points

*If you normally do nothing and you are bored and lonely, do something where you can meet like minded souls.

*Being happy is not a sin, it is your right.

Create Something

Creation of something is a powerful part of human existence. We gain a huge amount of pleasure from making something physical or mental. The following are suggestions for you to consider creating. Your mind might say that you lack the skills to do so but the attempt is important. We are not all poet laureates, bestselling authors, master mechanics or engineers but we do not need to be.

Build shelves or flat-pack furniture.

Fix a bicycle.

Paint a room of your house.

Write a poem about anything.

Write a story. As long as you have a start, middle and end you are an author.

Write your autobiography.

Write a biography of your parents or friends.

Make up a limerick. Short and to the point, clean or smutty.

Draw something, an apple or a landscape. Paint it if you want.

Take photographs of people, events, animals, nature and landscapes.

Think of your life and your dream life as a film.

Create a video for YouTube.

Learn to play a musical instrument.

Join a drama group.

Join a choir.

Offer help to people who need it.

Create a meal for an old person or a loved one.

Key Points

*Create something that makes you feel a sense of achievement.

*Your creations can be for yourself or others.

Mistakes

Adam once met a man who told him the following:

"There are people who make mistakes because they care. They are the good guys because they tried but got it wrong. They will try again until they get it right.

Then there are the people who make mistakes because they do not care. Get them out of your life. They will walk away from the mess and blame others. They will never try to get it right."

If there is somebody in your life who is messing up your right to feel content, let them walk away with their lack of care.

Because you are reading this book it shows that you do care. You care for yourself and you want to care for the wellbeing of others.

If you have made mistakes because you care then here you will find the guidance to put those errors behind you and move forward..

Your recipe is not ruined, it just needs a bit of tweaking to make it better.

Key Points

*We all make mistakes but some follow a lack of care and others are from being caring. Be one of the good folk.

Domination Control

Queen Bees and Hornets

There are people who are controlled in the name of 'love'.

There are mothers who want to live their lives through their children because their own lives were damaged. These matriarchs want to turn their daughters into models at very early ages. When I say models, that includes a physical representation of the perfect child brought up by the perfect mother (of course), or it could be a junior beauty queen (same motive) or a daughter who does not make the same mistakes in her choice of a partner so the mother inspects and rejects potential boyfriends. This control makes the children, the young adults and mature ones very unhappy and they find it hard to rebel for fear of hurting this queen bee in their lives.

If you are in this situation please do something to make YOUR life happy. You are not a puppy to be trained in obedience; you are a free roaming creation of life. If making yourself happy makes a controller unhappy then that is a problem of their own making.

Become free, resist the emotional blackmail that is part of the control technique and learn to be the only controller of your life and happiness.

Then there are male controllers and abusers. These are men, mostly fathers, who treat their children as sex toys. You have no options other than to report this to the appropriate authorities. If you are worried that you will get into trouble because nobody will believe you, please remember that there are experts who deal with these problems and they will assure you that you are not the only person to have been abused.

The same applies to physical, verbal and emotional abuse by a male or female partner.

These are issues beyond the scope of this book but there are many sources of help available.

Tribal Chiefs at Work

Work is where we find the tribal hierarchy that has been in existence for ever. There is a range of warriors that will be confident enough to train and help younger people to be allies and supports for their causes.

Then there are warriors that worry that the other employees bare threats to their position and will do what they can to pass on blame for their own mistakes. This weakens them because they lose allies and one day they will be challenged.

Warriors that worry about their place in a tribe (company) will work longer hours; will try to play political games that they will either win or lose or they will become rebels to upset the running order of the other players.

Do you remember the day you were offered your job. You went home full of pride and happy that you were needed.

If you have become discontented with it then it is time to review why that original feeling changed.

If you are unhappy at work appraise your position as if you were working out a playing strategy. Nominate the characters in your game and what their roles are.

Identify what the game is about and what the winning rules are.

If you can figure out a different way to play the game then you can find that content again. If not then perhaps now is the time to find a different company to work for. You know your strengths and weaknesses. Use them to recover your self-belief in your values to others.

Key Points

*Never be dominated. It does not matter who it is, your mother, father, siblings or bosses. Stand your ground. Stop abuse of any type from happening.

*Job evaluation happens by bosses. Allow yourself to evaluate how you feel about your work situation. Job satisfaction is vital.

Predators and Bullies

There might be some people who will regard you as weak because they are and they want to dominate to make themselves feel better. No chance.

They will have no contentment. These are predators of your emotional life and bullies of your very being and have to steal to make themselves feel better. Laugh them away.

From my garden I can watch big buzzards soaring in the sky on the wind. These can be bullies and try to predate on the young hatchlings of other birds. They are chased by magpies that resemble fighter planes chasing a big bomber. The buzzards are many times bigger than the magpies but they flap and fly hard to escape the smaller protectors. These are our role models for peace. When predators and bullies are stood up to they often run away. Using a smaller still example, watch the bully run from an angry wasp.

Be careful with physical bullies because they only know how to do damage to others but the emotional ones will give in. Remember, they are weak behind their seeming bravado.

Justice is contentment after a fashion.

Key Points

*Never let bullies win. The same with predators. They are all weak and puff themselves up to appear bigger than they are. They are more miserable than most.

Take Off Your Mask

We wear a variety of social masks that present what we want others to see in different situations. That is fine when we it happens naturally. In fact we are seldom aware of the different personas we show. However when we pretend to be what we cannot live up to then we have problems.

To be is better than seeming to be. Sometimes we wear disguises that we think cover up our weaknesses and by doing so we project our insecurities onto other people. Most masks are really transparent and can be seen through.

Be the person you are, be true to yourself. If you feel the need to pretend to be a different person then become that other person. Take on the real attributes that you are playing. There is an old saying that says that a good liar needs a good memory. When you become what you want to be than the truth is the only thing you have to remember.

We can pretend that we have a good life and that we have good relationships or that we are doing well at work but these are lies to other people and ourselves that will eventually become a burden.

Key Points

*Be true to yourself. Throw away any masks of deception that you wear.

*Become what you want to be by making an effort rather than pretending.

Criticism And Praise

The bad is always easier to spot than the good

Give praise where it is due. This motivates others who, in return, will respect your views and they will return good feelings to you.

Children, when they grow are not experts but praise for good efforts lead to better ones until they feel confident as young adults and thereafter.

In any relationship, personal or work-wise, praise is always more powerful and less destructive than criticism.

Words are strong weapons when used badly. As a specific issue that can be generalised into different scenarios, if your partner has put on weight then telling him/her that they are fat will count against you and will build a resentment that results in even more weight gain. If you want to encourage him/her to lose weight then offer praise for a change in eating habits or exercise regimes. Praise how good that person looked when they were slimmer without additional detail. The message is for motivation to become healthier.

In the work situation, an employee may lack motivation because their efforts are deemed to be less than they could be. Rather than criticisms and threats that they might be fired, your job as their boss is to train that person in the areas of expertise that they lack to make them more efficient. Going back to the example with children, if they cannot ride a bicycle the first few times they try, if you threaten to throw the bike away then that child will probably never learn to ride it. Praise their efforts, teach them well and they might become a Tour de France champion.

We are children in many respects, just older and bigger in our bodies.

Our minds are still receptive of criticism and praise.

If you feel you have been unfairly criticised then stand your ground calmly rather than ranting and raving. If you lose your temper then you set yourself up for more criticism. Take a breath, think about what was said and make your case.

If you are the object of unfair criticism then ask the critic how you can change and offer praise for their help (whether you mean it or not) and they will have to explain why they have been negative to you. Play the game so they will take the praise for helping you and they will then become your ally rather than your negative judge. Devious? Who cares?

Key Points

*Criticism is destructive.

*Praise is motivating and always welcome.

Social Mobility

If you have moved into different circles in your life and have become distanced from your friends and family by geography and/or money then you may have become discontented because your roots have become too distant.

The world has expanded and shrunk at the same time. I live in France, forty minutes from Bordeaux airport which is an hour and fifteen minutes away from my family in England. By that I mean that they live in very different parts of England and they are within easy reach of the four airports we can fly into.

There are telephones and Skype with which we can keep in touch. The distances from our home in England were shorter in miles but took longer to drive.

So people are within reach wherever you live but not just around the corner as they might have been a hundred years ago. We have to cope with what we have. There is a need to move for work that has to be balanced with the desire to keep in touch.

The keystone to dealing with a flux of family and friends is contact.

Key Points

*Keeping in touch is easy no matter how far away people are.

Imposing On Others

Wear metaphorical headphones!!!

Incoming

Your sense of peace can be ruined when others will not let you rest or work on your projects. They might not understand that you do not want to be disturbed so explain, ahead of what you want to do, that you would like some time on your own. Depending upon whom that person or people may be they might be suspicious of your motives. They need to know that what you are doing is decent and inoffensive. They regard their privacy as a right, perhaps. You can say that to them in the hope that they will understand.

Then there are people who want to impose their advice on you as if you are an idiot. Change the subject. Or you could thank them for their input but explain politely that you have thought the matter through and you have come to you own conclusions.

Outgoing

Never impose your tastes on others who do not wish to share them. These include sensitive topics such as sex, food, music, art, TV programmes, religion and so on.

If these topics arise then you can listen and comment but avoid preaching your viewpoint to others. See the effect in the 'incoming' section above. You will alienate people who do have the same ideas about contentious issues as yourself. You can discuss and debate them but never become a bigot with fixed opinions within a closed mind.

To close the metaphor above, wear metaphorical headphone and turn off your loudspeakers. Listen and broadcast at a comfortable volume.

Key Points

*Stop people from imposing their presence or views on you.

*Avoid imposing your presence or views on other people. Be able to calmly discuss topics.

Avoid

Avoid things in your life that are judgemental.

Television is full of trivial competitions that place ranks on skills and performance. Talent shows will show the poor but 'amusing' entrants because it fills space and makes people laugh at others. The socially inept people who appear on programmes such as Jeremy Kyle's are there to make the audience laugh at the problems of others whilst feeling good that the viewers are 'better' than the exhibits in the freak show.

Quiz shows hurt us because the knowledge that we have does not win us the huge amounts of prize money on offer.

Politicians bitch at each other and talk in terms of the other person's failure to bring miracles about. Contentment is not on their agenda. Discontent with their competition is what they need to gain votes.

It suggests that failure is normal.

The bottom line is that we become surrounded by negativity which sucks our contentment away.

Key Points

*Avoid being immersed in negativity where possible because it sets a low standard for our lives.

Procrastination

Stop making excuses for not doing something. Do it and the problem disappears.

Make lists of the things you have to do and tackle the least desirable one first. After that do the second thing and so on. Having done the jobs you least like then your motivation to do the rest will increase.

When your chores are up to date you will gain a sense of satisfaction.

In short, make a start with SOMETHING and enjoy the sense of fulfilment when you have finished. Hopefully somebody will notice and offer praise. If they do not then point out your achievement and feel good.

Key Points

*"My advice is to never do tomorrow what you can do today. Procrastination is the thief of time." Charles Dickens

Balancing Your Life

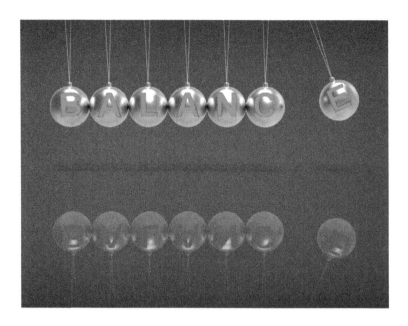

Is resolution of the balance of one or some of the following at the base of your lack of contentment?

Rather than skip through the A to Z lists on the following pages decide how each point might influence you and see if you can resolve some of your issues.

Not Enough:

Acknowledgement

When you make an effort for others either at work or in your private life it is good that you are acknowledged. Being taken for granted is hurtful and leads to bitterness which is the opposite of contentment. If your labours are worthy but not recognised then bring it to the attention of the person who lacks the politeness to notice. If that upsets them then it is sad but you are the person who has made the effort.

Balance

Do you give too much for no return? Do you receive too little from others? Balance is about equals on both sides. Communicate your concerns and discus your needs to make your life and the other person's life a happy and stable combination.

Compliments

Rather than looking for glowing praise for your work or appearance you can expect kind words for the way you are. If you give compliments then, very often, you will receive them in return. You can establish a culture of well-being that will be self-sustaining. Compare this with the example of a culture of insults where people will go to great lengths to create bad feelings when upset. They are verbal bullies. They feel better because they have become involved in a power game. If that can be applied to tributes then we will enjoy life better.

Confidence

Belief in yourself and your abilities is important. When you feel good about who you are and what you are able to you grow. How to start to build confidence when you believe that you lack it is a challenge but run a check on what you have in your favour.

Be like Superman. He was a weakling in his normal life, Clark Kent, but a superhero when he had to be. Identify which qualities you have that make you feel you are like Clark. Write them down. Then imagine what you would be like as Superman, the strengths you would have in talking to others, working, showing that super confidence. Change the original you into the super-you and then throw away the old you and block the way to return. Stand taller, straighter. Walk as if the world relied on you; talk as if you were a guru with faith in your words. Do this from this moment and, like magic, as long as you adopt the persona of the kind superhero then that is what you have become.

Contact

We are conceived from close contact and we grow up with it for food, love and social development. It is within our genes that we should seek out people, friends and family for company. Talk to others face to face, write, phone or Skype depending on proximity. They have as much need for contact as you do.

Love

Let us always meet each other with smile, for the smile is the beginning of love. Mother Teresa
Love isn't something you find. Love is something that finds you. Loretta Young

Whether you have lost love or you are seeking for it to grow or for it to come into your life, those two quotes sum up what is needed. You should put on a happy face to face the world and then people will see in you what they are seeking, a person to be at peace with and to share their feelings. Dream of love in your life and it will change your attitude towards suitors. They need to feel comfortable with you.

Money

There are two solutions, earn more and/or spend less. Earning more can be difficult in these lean times but if you feel comfortable in asking for a pay rise, do so. Changing jobs is an easy thing to say but difficult in reality. However keep your eyes and ears open for opportunities. If you do not then you will miss any chances that are available.

As for spending less it is a good idea to audit your outgoings. You can make small changes and those can add up to substantial amounts. For example, check your fridge to see how much you overbuy and throw away. Sometime two-for-one offers seem like value but are you consuming what you have bought? It is a good idea to think of your meal menus for the week and buy only the things you need for them. A good tip is to go to the supermarket on a full stomach because it reduces the urge for impulse buying. Other things you can do include walking or cycling more so that you drive less and spend less on fuel. Adjust your heating in winter to a lower level and wear warmer clothes.

It is not until you check on your spending that you can make those little savings that will add up.

Sex
If your partner has a very different sex drive to you then you need to seek a balance of needs by discussing what you both want as a solution. If this does not suit your partner or you and you cannot reach agreement then the problem will remain. Perhaps you will both need to seek help from a professional source but there will be an smattering of resentment from both of you. Agreement is easy if the love in the relationship is strong enough.

Time
Organise. Cut back on unnecessary usage of time. For example, clean the house less often. Nobody will notice anyway. Time can be made.

Likewise, with work ensure that you have equilibrium with the hours you spend earning your pay with the time you spend with your family and friends. Material gains are made worthless after emotional losses. If balance is kept then the search for wealth is fine but when the happiness of those people who love and should be loved is the real price, then is all the wealth in the world really worth it?

Too Much Or Many:

Anger
Aggression is dangerous. We have to look at anger from two sides. If you are an angry person then you need to seek help.

In a similar light, if you live with a person who suffers from anger then seek help. Anger can grow from bad words to physical injury. Ensure that you are in a safe relationship, please.

Criticism
Do you criticise too much? Do you feel disappointment rather than a failed attempt to do something right?

Are you the recipient of criticism?

In either case you must discuss the issue with the critic or ask yourself why you see catastrophe in the efforts of others.

Remember that criticism damages the ability to feel contented. I have a saying that is 'the most perfect thing about humans is our lack of perfection.' This drives us on to make progress. If the great inventors of the things in life that help us such as penicillin, the light bulb, X-Ray and so on fell victim to criticism, then where would we be?

Debt

Please read the **Money** heading above.

Drink, Drugs

Alcohol, cocaine, heroin etc. are ways to escape from an undesirable reality into a, perceived, better way of life.

If you have a problem with drink and/or drugs then sort out the issues that you are escaping from and ditto if your partner has a similar problem.

As with anger, drugs and alcohol destroy lives and relationships. Jail can beckon for theft or violence when the usual social norms are excluded. With younger people fired with alcohol and testosterone, the bestial drive to dominate and fight becomes paramount. This is seen with drugs such as cocaine as well as alcohol. Cocaine use leads to paranoia and this in turn, can lead to aggression.

Jealousy
Jealousy is said to be the third leading cause of non-accidental homicide across different cultures.

Unlike envy, a jealous person is worried that something they love, whether physical, personal or monetary, will be taken away by somebody who is perceived to be better. A jealous person might be envious of another but the jealousy is directed at what is considered to be the possession of the jealous person.

Sometimes a partner is causing it because of their infidelity or it is self-invented because of your lack of self esteem.

Loneliness
Negative emotions like loneliness, envy, and guilt have an important role to play in a happy life; they're big, flashing signs that something needs to change. Gretchen Rubin

See the heading **Contact** above. When you feel lonely you can either wallow in self-pity or do something about it. The first effort will pay you huge dividends.

Orders
Request rather than order actions and behaviours from others. They

will not feel threatened and will be much more likely to do as you ask with enthusiasm rather than resentment.

If you are being ordered around then accept that you are a person rather than a spare part. Explain that soldiers obey orders for the safety and protection of themselves and the others. Orders in your normal life are inappropriate and should be modified to requests that can be worked on.

Orders are telling you to do something with an assumed authority than is impolite. If you order somebody to stand up they will look puzzled and surprised but if you request that they stand up with an explanation then they will be more than willing to do so. Take this example with you as a response to anybody ordering you around.

Sexual demand on you.
There is a scale along which this topic runs from somebody asking to make love to a person asking you to do something that revolts you.

The first end of this scale can be discussed and agreement one way or the other reached. Perhaps tomorrow if you are feeling tired, maybe Saturday night and so on.

In the second case, depending upon the manner in which you are told to do something you do not want to do you can reply with, 'If you don't love me enough not to do that, then where does our relationship go?'

If the other person is too persistent then they have a major problem because they are only thinking of their own wants without consideration for you. Think long and hard about that relationship.

Time
Boredom. Do something. See the list of possibilities above in the section titled **THINGS TO DO.**

We can feel that we have too much time or too little. Swap and balance the two. Use the excess time to do the things you think you have too little time to do and vice versa.

Work
Organise your work load into things that have to be done straight away and prioritise the rest. Some tasks can be easily put out of the way by doing them or by putting them lower down your list of things to do.

Worry
Analyse why and then resolve those issues. These can include health See a doctor rather than worry. Once your issues have been recognised and treated then you can stop worrying.

Maybe it is wealth in which case set budgets that account for income and expenditure. Trim your money to your minimum needs. Easy to say, I hear you comment but the only other option is to live with the status quo and carry on worrying.

Happiness, or lack of it is perhaps the reason you read this book. Go back over the points and action them. Reading is pointless unless you commit to making positive changes.

Key Points

*Seek balance in your life. Avoid being negatively controlled and avoid controlling others.

*Control the amount of control that exists in your life either incoming or outgoing.

*Listen more than you talk. People will like you more.

*Sharing is a great way to gain happiness and friends. Two or more people in a joint enterprise makes it so much easier.

*Love making is sharing whereas sex for one person's relief is hurtful to a relationship.

*Look for contentment now and in the future. It is your life so do what makes you and others happy.

*You can train your mind to be positive and you can teach it to stop being miserable.

*Believe in your present and future wellbeing.

*Eliminate negative thoughts by eliminating negative words in your internal dialogue.

*Make positive affirmations about how you want to feel but apply them to the 'here and now'.

*Contentment is an emotional thing that never depends of the amount of money that you have. It is free.

*Selfish contentment will blow up in your face. Share the joys of life with others.

*Think about what you would need to feel really contented and then make that dream a reality by taking positive actions.

*Use your imagination to conjure up the emotional results you desire.

*Allow the events and people that will help you to achieve your dreams to enter your life and thinking.

*A great way to enjoy your thoughts is to take peace from your surroundings and mix them.

*Contemplation is a fast way to find relaxation.

*Surround yourself with friendly people.

*Keep in touch with your friends and family.

*Use social media if you find making face to face friends difficult.

*Be careful when contacting strangers. Some are not what they seem to be.

*If you normally do nothing and you are bored and lonely, do something where you can meet like minded souls.

*Being happy is not a sin, it is your right.

*Create something that makes you feel a sense of achievement.

*Your creations can be for yourself or others.

*We all make mistakes but some follow a lack of care and others are from being caring. Be one of the good folk.

*Never be dominated. It does not matter who it is, your mother, father, siblings or bosses. Stand your ground. Stop abuse of any type from happening.

*Job evaluation happens by bosses. Allow yourself to evaluate how you feel about your work situation. Job satisfaction is vital.

Never let bullies win. The same with predators. They are all weak and puff themselves up to appear bigger than they are. They are more miserable than most.

*Be true to yourself. Throw away any masks of deception that you wear.

*Become what you want to be by making an effort rather than pretending.

*Criticism is destructive.

*Praise is motivating and always welcome.

*Keeping in touch is easy no matter how far away people are.

*Stop people from imposing their presence or views on you.

*Avoid imposing your presence or views on other people. Be able to calmly discuss topics.

*"My advice is to never do tomorrow what you can do today. Procrastination is the thief of time." Charles Dickens

In Short

In short contentment and happiness depend on sharing and balance.

You have the ability to change. Discontent is a frame of mind that can be modified to result on contentment and happiness. All we have to do is make a start.

In your life there will be days when thunderstorms happen. They are short lived and the air clears. Never let an argument simmer in your mind. When the storm has passed return to your calm, contented and happy life.

Stop worrying and start to enjoy the life you have been given. Miracles are few and far between but making positive changes and holding on as tightly as you can to a positive attitude is of paramount importance.

Allow yourself to be happy. Nobody has cursed your life. You are the same as everybody else that has the choice between being miserable and being contented. They made the choice. Rather than following the paths of the unhappy people you meet use the joyful people as role models. Copy their beliefs and style.

Remember, stop worrying and start enjoying your life.

Reviews

If you have enjoyed this book and would recommend it to others or if you have any comments, please give a review when asked.

I would be grateful and very content if you would be kind enough to post a review. Thank you.

Other Publications by The Author:

Based on a huge amount of therapeutic work, these short stories, metaphors and interactive scripts can help you to bring about positive changes, eliminate negative thoughts and achieve your dreams.

Mind Changing Short Stories and Metaphors

Rather than being held back by old beliefs and attitudes the reader moves into a new way of thinking, a new way of acting and a new way of life. Some of the metaphors funny, some are dark. They tell tales of abuse and the nasty nature that some people have. However, the darkest hour is just before dawn.

Moving Forward

155

Short Stories
and Metaphors

by John Smale
author of
The Secret Language
of Hypnotherapy
Metaphors and stories for changing the
way we understand life, the World and
our feelings.

The stories are based on the adverse effects that behaviours, attitudes and actions have had on the lives of others. Therefore, if the readers can benefit from recognising symptoms of their own issues that have caused problems, then there is the possibility that they can take corrective action before suffering strikes them.

Short Stories and Metaphors